Essentially Soap

Robert S. McDaniel

Krause Publications
700 East State St., Iola, WI 54990-0001
Telephone 715-445-2214
www.krause.com

Please call or write for our free catalog of publications. Our toll-free number to place an order or obtain a free catalog is 800-258-0929 or please use our regular business telephone 715-445-2214 for editorial comment and further information.

Unless noted, photos are by Bob and Katie McDaniel or Krause Publications.
Cartoons are by Paul Malchow.

Library of Congress Catalog Number: 99-67694

ISBN: 0-87341-832-8

Printed in the United States of America

Acknowledgments

I suppose most authors must discover that their first project is much larger and harder than originally envisioned. I am no exception and wish to give special thanks to the people who supported me, physically, emotionally, and materially during the preparation of this book. I therefore offer special thanks to:

Jude, Joseph, Benedict, Michael, Therese, and Mary. You know why.

Lori, Deb, Butch, and Susan who offered samples, photography, and technical interaction; sometimes used, always appreciated.

Melody, Pamela, Kathy, Melanie, Graham, Marge, and Hannibal, my Internet friends and colleagues.

Kathie, sister, scholar, and speaker of ancient languages.

Paul and Sarah for the gift of shelter and kinship during final editing; and Paul for his cartoons.

Paul and Barbara at Krause for taking that chance and having patience with a new author.

And most of all to Katie for her unfailing support now and over the past 27 years.

Table of Contents

NTRODUCTION

"Tempus adest nunc," Rosmarus inquit, "multi loquendi: reges, caules, cothurnos, classem, sigillos. Cur mare si ferventius sestuat, sou subus alae."

("The time has come," the Walrus said, "to speak of many things, of shoes and ships and sealing wax, of cabbages and kings, and why the sea is boiling hot and whether pigs have wings.") Translation by K.M. Thomas.

I was a fat chemist for over 16 years. Personal issues aside, I did indeed work in the field of oleochemistry (fat chemistry) and specifically with emulsifiers and detergents from 1975 to 1991. Although I never worked for a company that made bars of soap, I worked with product and process development in emulsifiers, fabric softening agents, and detergents during this period, working with the "Big Three" - Proctor & Gamble, Colgate Palmolive, and Lever. Eventually, in the face of rampant buyouts and smart-sizing throughout the industry, I left for greener and more pleasant working pastures and became a technical manager with a company that makes and "converts" paper into various end products. A few years later, my wife strongly encouraged me to take up soapmaking as a craft. We had seen perhaps two soapmakers at various craft shows around the area and, as a former soapmaker, I thought I could first offer improvements in the basic product and then set out in unique directions of my own.

Today there are hundreds of cottage industry soapmakers throughout the world, making a few bars for friends or hundreds of pounds each week for the wholesale market. A guild for makers of handcrafted soap has been formed in the United States, and another is forming in Canada; and there are at least five soap lists on the Internet that bring together well over a thousand soapmakers of all levels of expertise, novice to professional, from around the world.

As my own work evolved, I found that my researches had to go well beyond soap. It was easy to find fragrance recipes, but fragrance is too personal for recipes unless you are trying to make an exact copy of something you like. I also found that the natural connection between soap and fragrances and functional additives was best described by literature dealing with the traditions of herbalism and the more modern area of aromatherapy. The ideas started to multiply seriously when a few people asked if I would be willing to demonstrate or offer workshops on soapmaking. I knew I couldn't recommend one single book as a resource, and I was somewhat concerned as to topics to discuss while I stirred my pot of soap. So the topics grew and grew, and I talked with more people and answered their really good questions and put that into writing. The result of all that stirring, thinking, and talking is the book you hold in your hands.

But as I started to say at the beginning, albeit in Latin, "The time has come to speak of many things..."

Robert L. McDaniel
"Dr. Bob"

CHAPTER 1
EARLY SOAP - ROCKS, ERUPTIONS, AND CHEMISTRY

The urge to clean seems to be as old as civilization. A variety of soapy materials have been used historically to clean our selves, our possessions, and our environment. The earliest substances were not true soaps but materials or chemicals (today called saponins) isolated from various plant sources. Initial usage was probably accidental, grabbing a handful of a saponin-containing plant along with the laundry at the edge of a stream. It wouldn't have taken much to realize that clothes didn't have to be pounded on the rocks quite so long whenever these plants were nearby.

In primitive locations soapwort or soaproot is still mashed up with water to produce a sudsy cleaning solution and modern science still has not identified a milder cleanser for ancient tapestries than the soapwort that was used when the fabric was newly made. (Of course, today ancient tapestries are more likely to be carefully cleaned using a toothbrush instead of the traditional rocks.)

Whatever the origin of soap, the first documented uses were certainly not for personal hygiene, but were for cleaning and processing hides and fleece. Practical soapmaking can be found mentioned on Sumarian clay tablets dating back to roughly 2500 B.C. The soap was produced from goat tallow and lye processed from the ashes of a native bush and was used to clean wool. In any event, by first century Rome, dye-containing soaps were used on hair (this fashion was borrowed from the Gauls), if not on other parts of the body.

According to one charming legend (completely unsupported by any hard evidence), the word "soap" purportedly is derived from Mount Sapo, a place where animals were burned in sacrifice to the gods, a common practice in ancient Rome. Rainwater naturally combined with the ashes from the altar, leaching out lye which combined and reacted with residual animal fat rendered by the heat from the fire; and together they trickled down the hill (forming soap as they went) into the river Tiber. Ordinary Romans found that their clothes washed cleaner in the sudsy water near the altars. And when you are beating your clothing on river rocks, getting them cleaner faster is important and noteworthy.

Another school of thought argues that soapmaking was Celtic (or from the Berbers in North Africa) in origin and brought back to Rome with the conquering legions and their spoils. Since anything non-Roman was considered barbaric, a legend was conveniently concocted demonstrating the Roman-ness of the invention of soap. Although the conflicting theories of the discovery of soap have not been sorted out, by the time Vesuvius erupted in 79 A.D., destroying Pompeii and Herculaneum, a soap factory was among the industries that were encapsulated for posterity by the ash. It is perhaps fitting then that the Roman poet Pliny the Younger, who is often considered the inventor of soap around 77 A.D., was among the surviving witnesses to the destruction of Pompeii. And, no matter who can claim credit for the invention of soap, the English word soap does in fact come from the Latin word for fat or grease.

All of which suggests that the Romans gloried in soapy bubbles in the public baths of the time - from the eternal city to Britain.

Roman poet and entrepreneur Pliny keeps his head and saves his soap as Vesuvius blows its top.

And, of course, it is just not true. As a matter of fact, even though Romans may have made and used soap for the laundry and various industries, they did not value soap for cleaning people. For personal hygiene, olive oil was massaged into the body, together with fine sand, and (for the wealthy) slaves wiped off the dirty oil with a squeegee-like device called a strigil. After this, a plunge into the public baths rinsed off the residue.

In a process related to traditional soapmaking, and one much less often mentioned, the Roman felt makers (fullones) used a form of soap to clean hides and fleece. In this industry, one lucky employee got to visit the inns at the various crossroads and collect urine in crocks. This was brought back to the workshop where it was poured into a shallow pit. Raw hides or fleece were then placed in the pit and another lucky employee got to hike up his toga, remove his sandals (hopefully), and spend the day walking over the hides and fleece in the pit. Of course, he was actually making soap, bringing the residual fat from the hides or the fatty lanolin from the fleece into contact with the ammonia from the urine, stirring it with his walking, and heating it with the hot Roman sun. In this way, the excess fat was removed, the process of felting was begun, and hides were softened and prepared for removing the residual hairs in the production of leather and parchments. This industry was odoriferous, though extremely profitable, and understandably often gave rise to complaints from the neighbors. However, these prosperous merchants were eventually taxed by the emperor; and Emperor Vespasian is cited as referring to them by stating, "pecunia non olet" or "money does not smell."

The Romans may not be able to claim the invention of soap, but their growing empire certainly began to spread the use and production of soap throughout the "civilized" world of Europe and into Africa. By the 8th century, soapmaking was common in Italy and Spain. In the 13th century, soap was introduced in France, where soap was commonly made from goat tallow and alkali (lye) from beech ash. Over the next century or two, the French devised a method of making soap from olive oil rather than animal fat, producing Castile soap, a far milder soap than previously known.

The French made at least three more key contributions to the development of soapmaking. It was the French who learned to make perfumed soap through the floral infusion of fat. Enfleurage, as it is known, is a multi-step process where fat is spread on a plank, then flowers or herbs are imbedded in the fat, leading to the extraction of the natural fragrance oil from the flowers into the fat. The process can be repeated several times to develop the desired intensity of fragrance. The scented fat can then be used in the production of scented soap or processed further (extracted into alcohol) to isolate the floral oils for use in perfumery.

No doubt the French would have dominated the world soap industry except for two things. First, of course, is that "luxury"

"Money may not smell; but if you ask me, this job stinks."

soaps (really meaning all soap designed for personal use) were a common target for royal taxes, which put most soap out of the reach of commoners. More importantly, in the mid-14th century personal bathing came to be considered highly dangerous. In the 1350s, the Black Death plague was pandemic. Of unknown origin, this invariably fatal disease was thought to be spread by noxious vapors, especially at night, and people who were damp from bathing were feared to be especially susceptible to catching this and other diseases. Although we know today that the plague is spread by fleas carried by rats, everyday life in European cities changed dramatically. Bathing became perhaps an annual event; windows, especially at night, were never opened; and in general personal hygiene suffered in favor of masking the odors with perfumes, scented handkerchiefs, floral and herbal bouquets, and the like. In fact, in the 1600s there is a report of four French thieves who were caught robbing the bodies of plague victims. The automatic sentence of death was not carried out when they disclosed that they avoided the plague by using an herbal concoction of absinthe, rosemary, sage, peppermint, rue, lavender, calamus, cinnamon, clove, nutmeg, and garlic all macerated together in vinegar with a bit of camphor.

In the early American colonies, most soap was made at home by boiling rendered animal fat with the alkali solution produced by treating hardwood ash with rain water. Wood ash was a common source of sodium and especially potassium hydroxides and carbonates, all forms of alkali. Rainwater was allowed to trickle through ashes, leaching out this lye mixture. A raw egg was often used to estimate the lye concentration: if the egg fell quickly through the lye, it was too weak and the solution was put back through the ashes to leach more alkali. If the egg floated on top, the lye was too concentrated and additional rainwater was added. If a more precise measure was desired, the concentration could be adjusted between batches so that the egg floated below the surface at a constant depth from batch to batch. Proportions were determined by observation on the hardness of the soap or by tasting the product to see that excess lye (which tingled on the tongue) was not present.

The soap produced by this method was a soft soap, usually stored in kegs. When the soapmaker wanted bar soap, she put the soap back in the kettle, boiled off more water, and added handfuls of salt, which converted some of the softer potassium soap into the hard sodium form. As you can see, soap-

A base of sand keeps ash and other solid impurities out of the lye.

Filled with ashes, the bucket is ready for water to leach the lye from the ashes.

Rain or other soft water is added and allowed to sit with the ash for about 24 hours to leach out the lye.

After 24 hours, the lye is ready to be captured.

The lye solution, filtered by the sand layer, trickles from the bucket.

The strength of the lye is tested by floating an egg: if the egg sinks, the lye solution is weak and it would be added to more ash to make a more concentrated solution.

When the egg floats at the top, the lye is strong enough for soapmaking.

making was more an art than a science at that time, and often the balance between lye and fat was not quite right, resulting in a harsh soap that was great for the laundry and kitchen floor, but left something to be desired when used on face, hands, and hair. The characteristic yellow color resulted both from color leached from the ashes and some rust from the cast iron cooking pots generally used for soapmaking.

The second key French contribution, and the most critical advance in soapmaking, occurred in 1791 when the French chemist LeBlanc invented a process to make sodium carbonate - soda ash - from salt by an electrolytic reaction. Lye could then be produced from the soda ash by calcining (heating) at high temperature. Suddenly a pure alkali, which enabled the production of nice hard bar soap, became widely available, independent of the availability of extensive hardwood forests. And finally, by 1823 the French chemist Chevreul determined the chemical nature of fats and detailed the chemistry of the process of soapmaking so that soap could be made by recipe with certainty, rather than by trial and error. This allowed for the large scale, controlled production of reproducible, mild soaps from locally available fats and oils. In other words, these discoveries led ultimately to the existence and successes of today's industry giants. And so, of course, they also led to our ability to make cold process soap.

CHAPTER 2
GLOSSARY

Don't panic! You don't need to know or understand all of these terms to successfully make soap. They are presented here in the event that you may run across some of them later in this book or when purchasing materials for your soapmaking.

ANTIOXIDANT A synthetic chemical or natural material that prevents or slows oxidation and rancidity in oils and soaps.

ABSOLUTE A fragrance extract made by extracting a concrete with alcohol.

ALDEHYDE A class of chemical compounds containing carbon, hydrogen, and oxygen. Aldehydes are more volatile and more reactive or unstable than alcohols, especially in the presence of strong alkali (lye).

AROMATHERAPY A theory that bodily health can be affected though the use of essential oils applied to the skin and/or inhaled to directly stimulate the brain to alter one's mental state or improve the healthful function of other bodily systems.

ASH a) A common term for a loose white layer that often forms at the surface of cold process soap, consisting of either sodium carbonate (from the reaction of lye with carbon dioxide from the air) or loose "beta" type soap crystals.

b) The residue from burning hardwood, from which a form of lye can be extracted.

CASTILE Olive oil based soap. The term is often used to describe both 100% olive oil based soap as well as soap made primarily, but not exclusively, with olive oil.

COLD PROCESS A process where fats and oils are converted to soap without cooking. Once the oils are heated to a desired temperature, a lye/water solution is added with stirring, and the oils are converted to soap plus glycerine.

COLORANT Natural or synthetic materials, such as dyes, pigments, and herbs, which are used to impart color to soap.

COMBAR Short for combination bar. Many commercial bar "soaps" are combinations of soap plus synthetic detergent.

CONCRETE A fragrance extract, usually of a flower, made by extracting the fragrance components into hexane or a similar organic solvent.

DETERGENT A blend of surfactants, usually synthetic, designed for cleaning, especially in the laundry. Also a synthetic surfactant.

DREADED ORANGE SPOTS Dark spots that form on the surface of soap caused by the oxidation of the component oils. Superfatted soaps are especially susceptible to this unless an antioxidant is added.

EMOLLIENT A material that has a soothing, softening effect on skin.

EMULSION A stable, non-separating suspension of oil in water or water in oil.

ENFLEURAGE A French term for the extraction of fragrance from flowers or herbs into oil.

ESSENTIAL OIL Essential oils are prepared from herbs and flowers either by steam distillation or by cold pressing (squeezing) oils from citrus peel. Essential oils are thought to have both mental and physical therapeutic effects.

ESTER A type of neutral compound formed by a condensation reaction between an acid and an alcohol. Chemically, fats and oils are esters of glycerine and fatty acids.

FAT Similar in composition to vegetable oils, but sourced from animals. Fats are neutral compounds (esters) of glycerine and fatty acids.

FATTY ACID An organic acid produced in plants and animals, usually containing an even number (at least eight) of carbon atoms. Chemically, a fatty acid is composed of carbon, hydrogen, and oxygen.

FATTY ALCOHOL A neutral fatty material containing an alcohol functional group. Most fatty alcohols are synthesized from fatty acid esters, though they occasionally occur in plants and animals.

FD&C Food, Drug, and Cosmetic. Materials listed as approved by the federal government for use in foods, drugs, or cosmetics.

GLYCERIN A natural three-carbon liquid sugar which forms the backbone of fats and oils.

GMS Goat milk soap.

GSE Grapefruit seed extract; thought to be an antioxidant.

HYDROPHILIC Water-loving. A hydrophilic material tends to absorb or dissolve in water.

INFUSION A tea-like extract of plant matter in either water or oil. Herbs and flowers are steeped or marinated in liquid to produce an infusion.

INS A term that relates an oil to the properties of soap made from that oil. INS relates to both the degree of unsaturation and the size (molecular weight) of the oil.

IODINE VALUE A measure of the unsaturation of a fat or oil. It is experimentally determined (measured).

KETONE A type of neutral organic compound containing a carbon-oxygen double bond. Ketones are fairly stable and usually more volatile than their corresponding alcohols.

KOH The chemical formula for potassium hydroxide.

LAURIC ACID A fatty acid 12 carbon atoms in length. Lauric acid soaps foam highly and readily dissolve grease and oil.

LINOLEIC ACID A polyunsaturated fatty acid, 18 carbon atoms in length. It is more unsaturated than linoleic acid and much more likely to oxidize and become rancid.

LIPID A fat or fatty material.

LIPOPHILIC Fat-loving. The fatty tails of a soap molecule are lipophilic, while the acid group at the "head" of the molecule is hydrophilic.

LYE The common name for sodium hydroxide. In the past it referred to natural alkaline material leached from wood ash and used to make soap; in that sense it can also refer to potassium hydroxide and its solutions.

LYE DEMAND The amount of lye needed to completely saponify a fat or oil.

LYE DISCOUNT The amount of lye omitted from a soap recipe in order to assure an excess of fat or oil (i.e. in order to superfat).

MELT AND POUR A type of soap, usually transparent, which when heated will melt and then solidify again upon cooling. Often seen shortened to M&P.

MYRISTIC ACID A fatty acid, 14 carbon atoms in length. Together with the 12-carbon lauric acid, it is primarily responsible for lather production in soap.

NaOH Sodium hydroxide - ordinary lye.

OCCLUSIVE Blocking the evaporation of water, usually from the skin.

OIL Triglyceride (compound comprised of glycerine and fatty acids) from vegetable sources.

OLEIC ACID An 18-carbon (length) fatty acid with a single double bond (unsaturation). The chief fatty acid in olive oil.

OLEFIN A generic term for organic compounds, hydrocarbons, which are unsaturated (have at least one carbon-carbon double bond in the molecule).

OXIDATION A chemical reaction with oxygen. Rust is an oxidation product of iron; rancidity or orange spots are caused by the oxidation of polyunsaturated fatty acids.

PALMITIC ACID Fully saturated fatty acid, 16 carbons in length. The main fatty acid in palm oil.

pH A scale, from 0 to 14, which measures the acidity or alkalinity of water. A pH of 7 is neutral, below 7 is acidic, above is alkaline.

PHOTOTOXIC Causing a toxic reaction, usually on the skin, when exposed to sunlight.

PIGMENT Natural or synthetic inorganic colors, often oxides of metallic elements.

POLYMORPH(IC) One of several naturally occurring crystalline structures of the same material, often exhibiting dissimilar physical properties.

POLYUNSATURATED Having more than a single carbon-carbon double bond in a molecule. Polyunsaturated oils are more liquid (have a lower freezing point) than saturated oils and also more prone to oxidation. Linseed oil, highly polyunsaturated, can cause fires when left exposed to air due to the heat liberated by air oxidation.

RANCID Degraded by oxidation. In the extreme case, oils become cloudy and smelly due to air oxidation.

REBATCHING Preparation of soap by redissolving freshly made soap in water or milk and allowing it to crystallize again.

RICINOLEIC ACID Unique to castor oil, this 18-carbon fatty acid is monounsaturated (like oleic) with an additional alcohol functional group along the chain.

ROE Rosemary oil extract. A fat-soluble antioxidant extracted from rosemary with proven antioxidant applications.

SAPONIFICATION The chemical reaction between lye and fats or oils, yielding soap and glycerin as the products of the reaction.

SAP Short for saponification value. The amount of lye required to completely saponify a specific amount of fat or oil.

SCFE Super critical fluid extraction. The process of extracting fragrant material from flowers or herbs using liquefied carbon dioxide (under high pressure).

SACCHARIDE A sugar or carbohydrate.

SEIZE Rapid solidification of a soapmaking reaction, often forming cottage-cheese-like "globs" of soap before it can be transferred into the intended molds.

SENSITIZER A chemical in a mixture that can cause an individual to develop allergic reactions to other materials in the same mixture.

SOAP The sodium (or potassium) salt of a fatty acid. Soap is prepared either by the direct reaction of fatty acids with lye or by

the reaction of lye with fats and oils (producing soap together with glycerin).

STEARIC ACID Fully saturated fatty acid, 18 carbon atoms in length.

STEROL A fairly high molecular weight natural alcohol; cholesterol is the chief sterol from animals and sitosterol from vegetable sources. They are similar in composition to sebum, a natural protective "grease" in skin and hair.

SURFACTANT A surface active agent; the general term for a material that reduces the surface tension of water (i.e. increases the ability of water to wet a solid placed in it). Soaps and detergents are all surfactants.

SUPERFAT Addition of excess fat or oil to soap. The process of making soap with an excess of fat or oil.

SYNDET A commercial bar "soap" containing only synthetic detergents, rather than soap.

TOCOPHEROL Any of several natural forms of Vitamin E.

TRACE The point at which a batch of soap is thick enough to pour into molds; when it is thick enough to resist separating back into oil and water layers. Trace is the point when a spoonful of the mixture, poured back into the pot, leaves a brief, faint imprint on the surface.

TRIGLYCERIDE A neutral compound consisting of one molecule of glycerin combined with three molecules of fatty acid. Fats and oils are triglycerides.

UNSAPONIFIABLE Literally incapable of forming soap by saponification. Unsaponifiables are primarily tocopherols and sterols, natural emollients which soften skin.

UNSATURATION Reactive sites in fatty acids and other organic molecules that have less than the complete amount of hydrogen. The presence of unsaturation makes an oil more liquid (lowers the temperature at which it solidifies) and its soap somewhat softer. Unsaturated oils are thought to penetrate the skin and are thus often used in cosmetic creams and moisturizers.

VISCOSITY Actually a term for resistance to flow. For example, honey is more viscous than water. An extremely viscous liquid can hardly be poured from one container to another.

WAX An organic neutral molecule that consists of a fatty acid reacted with or attached to a fatty alcohol. Although jojoba "oil" is a wax, most waxes are solids at room temperature.

WAX ESTER A wax. A compound similar in structure to a wax.

CHAPTER 3
NO LYE SOAPMAKING - MELT AND POUR AND REBATCHING

There is something inherently satisfying about making soap. Maybe it relates to the 4,500+ year history of human soapmaking; maybe it simply reflects a desire to keep the jungle at bay and put our stamp on our personal environment. For pioneer women, soapmaking was an annual event, often lasting days while lye was leached from wood ashes saved from the winter fires and then cooked with fat as the spring thaw began.

FOUR WAYS TO MAKE SOAP

Today soapmaking is much simpler and there are four main options available: **melt and pour**, **rebatching**, **cold process**, and the traditional **hot or boiled process**. Melt and pour is the easiest and involves doing just what it sounds like - melting and pouring. See page 20 for instructions. Rebatching is a tiny bit more complicated and is discussed on page 26. Cold process is the heart of this book and the instructions for this way of making soap begin on page 48.

The hot process, of course, refers to cooked soap, where the fat and lye/water solutions are boiled together until most of the water has evaporated and the resulting soap quickly solidifies on cooling. The hot process is used extensively by those involved in reenactments, Renaissance fairs, and similar demonstrations of the ancient art of soapmaking, though only the hardiest soapmakers still use lye leached from ashes.

In the cold process, the oil is first heated to the desired temperature and once the lye/water is added, no further heating is needed - the chemical reaction of saponification proceeds and generates sufficient heat until the thickened soap stock is ready to be poured into molds to solidify. Cold process soap offers a great deal of flexibility in the selection and use of fats and oils, colorants, and fragrances. Cold processing is the principle process used to make soap at home for those very reasons.

There are dangers of course. Lye, an essential chemical part for converting fat or oil to soap, is extremely hazardous, a corrosive, and poison. Making soap "from scratch" with children, animals, and spouses underfoot is not appropriate for most people. Saponification, the chemical process that converts oils and fats to soap, requires special equipment to measure ingredients and

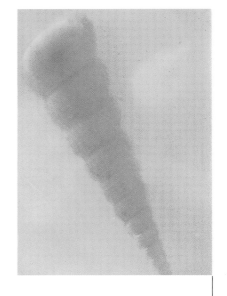

contain the reacting ingredients as well as specific personal equipment to assure the safety of the soapmaker and family.

But for those of us with the creative urge to hand-make something a cut above the mass-produced - something milder and more moisturizing and luxurious, something that exactly fits our conception of soapiness while avoiding the chemical hazards of saponification – there is a way. Or more precisely, there are two ways: 1) melt and pour, and 2) rebatched (often called hand-milled) soaps. Both melt and pour and rebatched soap start with pre-made soap that can be easily purchased ready to use.

MELT AND POUR SOAP

Melt and pour soap (often simply called M&P) is made with special, and usually secret, ingredients that allow it to easily melt in a microwave oven or in a pan of hot water so you can add your own special ingredients and let it solidify again. Melt and pour base soap is generally transparent and is usually purchased by the pound at various hobby stores and discount department stores. It is very easy to use and is suitable for simple kids' projects, requiring the same sort of supervision necessary for baking cookies. Other than its ease of use, the major advantage of melt and pour soap is the ability to produce striking visual effects by layering and embedding different colors and objects. This is the easiest soap to use for layering. The major disadvantage is in not knowing anything about the basic soap ingredients, since some melt and pours contain various organic solvents and chemicals that enable it to re-melt. It is, however, the best soap for kids' projects and since it is transparent it allows for enormous creativity in design. Many professional home soapmakers use melt and pour exclusively.

MELT AND POUR MAGIC

For melt and pour soapmaking, the necessary equipment is simple: melt and pour soap base, a heat resistant container (usually glass) for melting the soap, a mold (usually plastic) for the finished soap, color and fragrance, and a pan of hot water into which water and the glass container can be placed. A microwave oven can be used in place of the pan of water.

You can find a wide variety of molds that can be used for all types of soap. Candy molds - available at virtually any craft or hobby

Two red melt and pour soaps. One was formed using a powdered red dye for a rich uniform carmine color. The second bar started with a partially solidified melt and pour layer, half filling the mold, colored with a pearlescent pigment. When this layer started to solidify, a plain red colored layer was added to fill the mold. The result, seen here, is a swirled red pearlescent soap with a lighter top. When I started playing with the pearlescent and colored mica pigments in melt and pour, this was my favorite effect.

Clear colorless melt and pour base comes in a variety of shapes and is easy to cut into manageable pieces.

All the equipment needed for making melt and pour soap - and if you use a microwave oven, you don't even need the pan.

With a little preparation by the adults, melt and pour soap can be great fun for kids!

Finished bar of melt and pour, with color and scent added.

Just a few of the many color concentrates available for melt and pour: yellow, green, blue, and shocking pink.

And of course they can be mixed to produce other shades.

shop - can produce small fancy soaps for the powder room. Round, rectangular, and fancy shapes are also available in many craft stores and from soap suppliers (see supplier list) by mail or Internet order. Clean, dry plastic molds are the best since the flexibility of plastic makes it much easier to remove the finished soap from the mold.

FD&C (Food Drug & Cosmetic use approved) dyes are the colorants of choice for melt and pour soap. Powdered dyes are available for large batches of soap, but the most convenient forms to use are dye concentrates, usually called color tabs or color nuggets, where the color has been partially diluted in a melt and pour soap base. Each supplier offers their own suggestions as to how much to use for a pound of soap, depending on the depth of color desired.

FAQ

CAN I USE CRAYONS TO COLOR SOAP?

I am often asked about the feasibility of using crayons to color soap. My response is to suggest that you probably don't want to put something in soap that you wouldn't want to use directly on your skin. FD&C approved pigments and dyes are commonly used in makeup and related cosmetic preparations. Crayons are designed for use on paper, and as I recall, were rather hard to remove from children's skin. I would suggest using only herbs and FD&C approved colors in soap.

The final optional ingredient is fragrance. Essential oils, derived from herbs and flowers, are usually available from health and nutrition stores as well as from soap and aromatherapy suppliers. Fragrance oils are available from many of the same sources. A good starting point for scent addition is 1/2 teaspoon of essential oil or one teaspoon of fragrance oil per pound of soap, added to the melted soap just before pouring it into the mold.

Ready for the microwave; it will only take a few 20 second bursts on full power to melt.

With parental supervision, melt and pour is a great project for ages five and up. Smaller children also like this process, but can get bored waiting between steps.

STEP-BY-STEPS FOR MELT AND POUR IN THE MICROWAVE

Yield: 4 to 8 ounce batch of soap (1 to 3 bars)

1. Slice a piece of melt and pour base soap into approximately 1/2" to 1" cubes, and place them in the glass container.
2. Slice a piece of soap color and add it to the container with the soap.
3. Heat the soap on full power for 30 seconds, and check to see if it is completely melted. Repeat until the soap is completely liquefied (melted).
4. Add the desired amount of fragrance oil and stir.
5. If you want your soap to be a uniform color, stir the soap with a spoon or small whisk until the color is even. (For other color effects, see Making It Personal on page 21.)
6. Carefully pour the soap into the mold and leave at room temperature for an hour or until solid.
7. Turn the mold upside down and gently twist or push on the bottom to release the soap. If the soap does not come out easily, refrigerate or freeze it for an hour and try again. You can also pour a little warm water on the inverted mold (or dip the mold briefly in a pan of warm water) to help the soap slide out of the mold.
8. Immediately wrap the finished soap in plastic wrap or place it in a plastic bag or similar container. Left open, it will pick up moisture from the air and become cloudy over time.

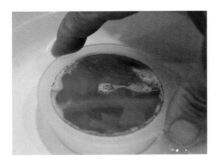

Place the filled mold in warm water to loosen the soap.

Gently warmed, the soap pops out of the mold with minimum effort.

Although the soap in the middle is made of layers of blue and pink, the resulting visual effect, seen through both layers, is quite different. A good lesson that blue and red make purple.

MAKING IT PERSONAL: FRAGRANCE, COLOR, AND STYLE

Melt and pour soap lends itself to creative visual techniques because it is transparent and because, through the use of dyes, striking colors can be achieved. Even the pigment colors commonly preferred for cold process soap can be used to give interesting effects, though much of the brilliance of the color is lost. When you add scent, you add another dimension to your creation. Since it is so very easy to handle melt and pour, you can blend colors, scents, and visual effects with striking results.

Layered soaps can be produced by pouring a layer of one color, letting the layer cool until it thickens (normally five to ten minutes will suffice), and then pouring a second layer of a different color (and scent). This process can be repeated to form a series of colored layers. The first layer is not ordinarily allowed to completely solidify or the different layers may not stick together in

the finished soap. If the layers don't stick together sufficiently, a small amount of alcohol (either grain alcohol or rubbing alcohol) can be sprayed or brushed on the surface of the first layer prior to pouring subsequent layers to help the layers stick together.

Melt and pour colored with pigment containing mica sparkles; interesting effects result, but clarity and depth of color is lost.

WHY CAN'T I MAKE A SOLID WHITE BAR OF SOAP AS EASILY AS I CAN MAKE THE TRANSPARENT MELT AND POUR TYPES?

Take heart, now you can. Quite recently, opaque white melt and pour soap has come onto the market. It comes in the same form as transparent melt and pour - blocks or slabs - and melts just as easily. You can use dyes and pigments to color it if you like. Check with hobby shops and soap suppliers to see if they carry it.

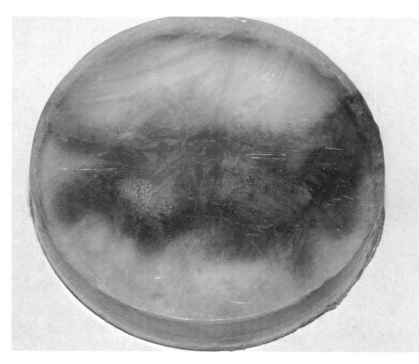

There are many ways to get special visual effects by partially mixing colors.

Variegated colors result from mixing types and colors of soap. Cold process soap can be added through melt and pour or just placed in the middle, between layers.

Swirls and marble effects can be obtained by adding a small amount of a darker color and dragging it through the initial melted soap, using a fork, chopstick, or small whisk. The extent of the effect can be varied by forming subsequent layers without allowing the initial layers to thicken appreciably and then partially mixing the layers.

Variegated soaps can also be made by forming cubes of colored soap, thoroughly chilling them so they don't melt appreciably when hot soap is poured over them, and imbedding them in a mold full of clear melt and pour. Of course, the imbedded soap does not have to be melt and pour, any colored soap can be used. In fact, the primary difficulty in imbedding melt and pour soap is the tendency of the imbedded soap to partially melt into the surrounding soap. However, since cold process soap resists melting, it is often easier to use chunks of ordinary cold process soaps to create these effects.

First a thin layer of base soap is poured and allowed to thicken.

Chunks of opaque soap are scattered atop the first layer and gently pressed into the bottom layer.

Additional melt and pour is poured to completely fill the mold.

The filled mold ready to release the soap.

The finished soap.

Another interesting effect can be produced by using a cookie cutter to cut a figure out of dark soap and imbedding this chilled figure into the center of a bar of clear melt and pour. Depending on the melting temperature of the soap, it may be necessary to chill the imbedded soap in the freezer prior to using, to avoid appreciable melting. When you are forming layers, though, freezing one layer will not permit good adhesion with the next layer. You can also take advantage of another feature of the various melt and pour soap bases, since the more transparent soaps are softer than the translucent varieties. Thus you can use a lower melting transparent soap in combination with a more colored and harder translucent soap to avoid intermingling the colors.

Colored melt and pour being poured onto a plastic lid, ready to form shapes. It would have been much easier if I had covered the lid with plastic wrap before pouring the soap layer.

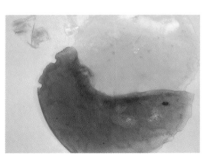

Cookie cutters forming the shapes that will be imbedded between layers of melt and pour. The shapes should be chilled in the refrigerator before use to avoid melting when in contact with the hot melt and pour.

Kids love the shapes and will happily choose their own color, shape, or fragrance for the center of their very own soap.

You can avoid the melting issue altogether by imbedding sea shells or flat rubber toys. The only problem in handling small rubber toys is that they may try to float to the top of the mold instead of staying where you want them. If this happens, use a toothpick to push the toy back to the center of the mold until the melt and pour hardens enough to trap it where you want it. Seashells are usually heavy enough so they don't float and are easier to handle. In all cases when you use toys in soap, remember that they can be a choking hazard for small children.

Multi-layered soaps can also be made more interesting by the judi-cious combination of fragrances, especially those reflecting the color selection. Layers of pink strawberry or raspberry alternating with creamy vanilla or dark choc-olate; a red cherry layer on top of a white chocolate layer; a layer of violet lavender over a pinkish rose - all are examples of fragrance combinations reinforcing the visual impact. Although the same approach could be taken with chunks of one fragrance imbedded in another, the fragrance of the smaller pieces will often get lost and in that case, it is often more effective to combine the fragrances rather than to keep them separate.

Three types of objects imbedded: a plastic fly, seashells, and a large irregu-lar chunk of clear melt and pour.

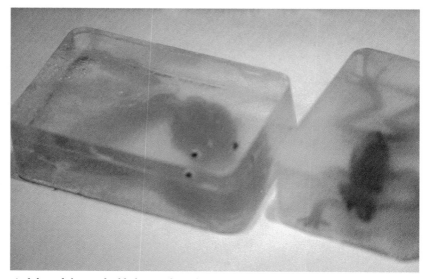

A fish and frog imbedded in melt and pour. Remember to place the objects upside down in the mold, since the smoothest (top) side of the soap will be against the bottom of the mold!

Kids love fragrances that match the colors: lemon yellow, mint green, blueberry, and strawberry complement the selected colors.

FAQ

I SAW SOME TRANSPARENT SOAP LOAVES WITH RODS OF COLORED SOAP RUNNING THROUGH THEM. CAN I DO THIS TOO?

Certainly you can do this. The process starts with a mold in the shape of a round cylinder. A smooth sided can will do nicely. First get a wood or preferably metal dowel or rod, 3/4" to 1" in diameter, and stand it in the center of the cylinder. The rod should be coated with oil or a release agent such as used for candles. Then pour the outer shell of melt and pour into the mold around the rod. When the soap has completely set, remove the rod by carefully twisting as you pull it out. The round cavity that results can be filled with a different color of melt and pour soap. This process can be applied to a loaf as well, but there you have to put the rod in the center of the soap and cut part of the soap away to expose the rod and make the hole.

WHAT DOES THE TERM HAND-MILLED MEAN?

Milling is a common industrial term that basically means "ground." So hand-milled soap is soap that is ground (or grated) by hand, then reassembled into bar form. Ground or grated soap is easier to dissolve in water or milk than a big lump. There is no real difference between hand-milled and rebatched soap; it is just a matter of semantics.

REBATCHED SOAP

Rebatched soap is an easy-to-use form of cold process soap. In fact, rebatched starts with cold process soap that is only a day or two old, sealed in plastic bags, and still fresh enough to retain a high water content. This new soap is shredded or extruded into what are typically called soap noodles. Although some soapmakers rebatch all their cold process soap, many simply buy the packaged noodles from a supplier. Since the base is often available in a variety of raw ingredients (100% olive, mostly olive, lard/coconut blends, etc.) the soapmaker can make a variety of soaps without having to handle lye at all. An additional advantage of rebatching is the ability to make or buy large batches of cold process soap and convert it into many special colors, scents, shapes, etc. - something that is often difficult to do directly with a large batch of cold process soap.

The process of rebatching the soap requires adding water, or more typically milk, to the noodles and heating the mixture to about the boiling point of water

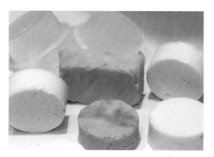

Color effects can be varied with rebatched soap, depending on when the color is added.

to redissolve the soap. Soap can be rebatched in a crock pot, double boiler, or in a covered casserole dish using a microwave or conventional oven.

REBATCHING WITH SOAP NOODLES

Soap noodles in a casserole dish with a color tab; ready to process.

Many of the same decorative techniques used for melt and pour soaps can be applied to rebatched or hand-milled soaps. Although you can make your own cold process soap base, it's also available ready-to-use from a number of suppliers in the form of soap noodles. These noodles are soap, usually high in olive oil, that has not been left in the open to cure and lose moisture. Instead, usually within 24 hours of saponification, the soap is grated, extruded in a meat grinder, or chopped in a food mill and immediately placed in a plastic bag to prevent water loss and retain the initial plasticity of the soap. When the soap is completely melted, oils, fragrances, herbs, and color can be added before the soap is put into a mold to harden.

Why rebatch? Since the soap is already made, you do not have to handle lye. Furthermore, you can add ingredients that are not stable under the highly alkaline conditions present during the initial soapmaking process. For those wanting to produce a soap using aromatherapy essential oils, rebatched soap will retain all essential oil components except those that are not stable to, or evaporate at, the temperatures required to melt the soap. Herbs may also be added to the melted soap with substantially less discoloration than when added to cold process soap. And, since milk is easier to use in this process than water, this is a very simple way to make goat's milk soap, which is noted for its silky feel. In general, whole milk from any source or fresh or reconstituted powdered milk will more easily dissolve the soap noodles than will reduced fat milk, which in turn will work better than plain water.

Typically, when you purchase soap designed for rebatching, the supplier will offer instructions for the appropriate temperature and amount of liquid to add to their particular recipe. Soap can be rebatched in a double boiler, a crock pot set to low, or in a covered pot or dish in the oven, with the oven temperature set at 200°F to 225°F. In general, a typical starting point is to add a scant 1/2 cup of room temperature or slightly warm whole milk to each pound of fresh soap noodles (or your own freshly made and ground cold process soap). To give you a feel for volumes, a two-quart covered casserole will hold approximately 2-1/2 pounds of soap noodles and 1-1/4 cups of whole milk with sufficient room to add additional liquid if needed.

Cover the casserole, then heat this mixture at 220°F to 250°F for one to three hours to produce a thick soap "soup." Since the mixture is not always smooth at this point, a little mixing with a small whisk or hand blender can help the melting process to form a uniform soup. If the soap is still not dissolving or melting, add another 1/2 cup of warm milk or water for each pound of soap noodles. Be careful not to add too much liquid or it will take much longer for the soap to solidify enough to be removed from the mold.

As the soap is melting, it often speeds up the process if you stir it up by hand.

Additional color can be added at any stage along the way and blended in.

When the thick rebatched soap has melted to the point where it has no obvious solid chunks remaining, add colorants (see below), fragrances, special oils, or ground herbs and mix well. Pour the soap into a mold. Note that due to the high temperatures involved in this process, some fragrance will be lost to evapora-tion (the lighter the fragrance, the more will be lost). A good starting point for scent addition is to add 1/2 ounce of essential oil or one to two ounces of fragrance oil for every two to three pounds of soap noodles.

I have found that a very simple way to make small batches (up to two pounds) of rebatched soap is in the microwave oven. Place one to 1-1/2 pounds of soap noodles in a small glass casserole dish, add 1/2 cup of tepid whole milk, cover the dish, and place it in the micro-wave. Heat on full power for 60 seconds and examine the contents to see how far the soap has melted. (Since microwave ovens vary in power or strength, you must gauge the length of cooking time for your particular oven.) Continue to heat in 60 second intervals until an appreciable amount of the soap has melted, then add coloring and use a fork to stir the soap (to help it melt uniformly). Continue heating in 60 second cycles and add about 1 tablespoon of milk between cycles until the soap is a uniform consistency - usually more spoonable than pourable. When the soap has reached this uniform, thick but spoonable stage, stir in about one teaspoon of

This rebatched soap is thick enough to use a rubber spatula to fill the molds.

your desired fragrance oil and use a spoon, ladle, or rubber kitchen spatula to transfer your now scented soap into a mold.

As an alternative to using a mold, as the rebatched soap cools down, you can easily roll bits of soap in your hands to make soap balls. If you wet your hands, the soap will not be as sticky. Although the soap balls tend to collapse a bit as they cool and age, you can re-roll them in your hands after a few hours to keep them round.

When the rebatched soap cools enough, you can roll it into balls. Be sure to slightly wet your hands with water to keep it from sticking.

The ball will deform a bit while the soap is still soft, but you can re-roll it the next day to keep it round.

Soap rebatched this way will normally be ready to remove from the mold in six to 12 hours. Larger batches, which are thinner due to the addition of extra milk, may take as long as a few days to solid-ify sufficiently to remove from the mold, though often it is helpful to freeze it first to make unmolding easier. It is important to lightly press on the soap (poke it gently) to determine that it is solid enough to hold its shape when removed from the mold. Although rebatched soap does not need to cure (there is no unreacted lye or incomplete chemical reaction in the soap), it still needs to rest open to the air for three to five weeks so any excess water will evaporate and it will harden to a usable state. If used prematurely, the rebatched soap will tend to dissolve too quickly in water.

Frozen soap in a mold is warmed in a bowl of hot water.

After 10 to 15 seconds in hot water, the soap will easily come out of the mold.

Like melt and pour, rebatched soap can be formed into layers, though the effect may not be as striking as with melt and pour soaps. To layer rebatched soap, simply half fill the mold with the original layer and as soon as this layer has thickened to where it is

soft but solid, add the second layer. Alternately, contrasting colored and scented soap can be spread or dribbled on top of the original batch of soap, in a fashion similar to frosting a cake.

Color uniformity in rebatched soaps can vary with the type of colorant used and when it is added. Adding water-soluble dyes to the milk or water prior to starting rebatching will ordinarily produce a uniform color. If you use any of the various color tabs - a concentrate of soap and dye - you can achieve a marbleized effect by adding the color tab when the soap is nearly dissolved, but still thick. The earlier a color tab is added, the more uniform the color

Chocolate scented soap with coconut scented white and dark soap as "frosting."

Layered soap formed by dividing the soap batch and using different colors. You don't have to scent the layers differently, though that adds to the "scentsation."

will be. I must also point out that color often intensifies in rebatched soap, especially when color tabs are used. So don't be surprised when that pale lavender becomes darker in a day or two.

When color is added just before transferring the soap into a mold, the color usually comes out in streaks and swirls, but when added from the beginning a more uniform color results.

Although the rebatching technique can also be used to recover batches of cold process soap that are cosmetically challenged (ugly), or that don't have the desired fragrance, many people routinely rebatch almost all their handmade soap. Some prefer the texture of rebatched soap, while others want to be absolutely certain that all the ingredients are thoroughly reacted. In any case, though some soapmakers may refer to rebatching as something done to save a batch of soap and hand-milling as an intentional or planned operation, the distinction has no basis in fact - either term may be used, no matter what the original intentions were.

Butterfly soap from a plastic hobby mold.

CHAPTER 4
LUXURIOUS COLD PROCESS SOAP-
WHY TO MAKE YOUR OWN

After a while, it all comes down to the question: WHY? Why make soap when you can buy it at the grocery store? The answer, or at least my answer, describes the wonderful nature of cold process soap.

⬚ COLD PROCESS SOAP RETAINS ALL THE NATURAL GLYCERIN in the soap, unlike most commercial bars. Glycerin is a natural emollient that dramatically boosts lather and provides a milder soap that is gentler to the skin. Glycerin is removed from commercial bars since it is a valuable chemical in its own right – more valuable than the soap.

⬚ COLD PROCESS SOAP IS FORMULATED FOR YOU. A balanced combination of coconut, palm, olive, soy, and canola (or your other favorite) oils produce a superior soap. You don't have to make a large profit at 50 cents a bar using only cheap ingredients in the most economical recipes. Coconut oil gives superior lather, palm oil or vegetable shortening makes for a harder, longer lasting bar, olive, canola, and lard are especially mild and skin nourishing components. Superior performance costs more.

⬚ EACH RECIPE IS UNIQUE. It bears repeating that the recipes need not change whenever coconut oil increases in price by a nickel.

⬚ Many people want to make an all-vegetable soap, free of animal products and without animal testing (except for family and friends). *When you make the soap, you have total control over the ingredients.*

⬚ MANY COMMERCIAL "SOAPS" ARE ACTUALLY DETERGENT BARS - they are based on synthetic detergents instead of all natural ingredients. Synthetics can be harsher to your skin than natural soap, especially without the natural glycerin.

This is what it is all about - you are making the soap just the way you want it.

◈ COLD PROCESS SOAPS CAN BE MADE WITH THE SAME COSTLY EMOLLIENTS USED IN THE FINEST COSMETIC LOTIONS AND CREAMS - cocoa butter, shea butter from the African karite tree, our native jojoba oil, beeswax, milk and milk solids, oatmeal, and honey - all natural ingredients included for their superior mildness and moisturizing properties.

◈ YOU CONTROL THE CHOICE OF COLORANTS AND FRAGRANCES. Most people who are allergic to soaps and detergents are actually allergic to the colorants and/or the synthetic fragrances. Colors and fragrances can be selected from herbs, natural or high tech synthetic pigments, essential oils steam-distilled from herbs, and high quality fragrance oils. Selections based on herbal medicine and aromatherapy can result in product(s) that have beneficial properties as well as a pleasing fragrance and a long history of safe use among humans. Many of the essential oils often used require hundreds of pounds of herbs to produce a single pound of essential oil.

◈ COLD PROCESS SOAPS ARE LONG LASTING. A properly designed cold process soap will last as long as a commercial soap bar, and longer than many brands.

◈ I PERSONALLY MAKE MY SOAP - HAND-CRAFTING EACH BAR, watching and assuring the quality of starting materials and finished products. I age my soaps for almost a full month, and sometimes longer, before I consider them ready to sell and use. This assures the quality and mildness I have designed into my product.

◈ MY NAME AND REPUTATION ARE PART OF MY PRODUCT just as surely as the vegetable oils I use. If you should have a problem with my hand-crafted soap, I am here; I am not a nameless, faceless cog in a huge corporation. I am proud of my soap and happy to please my customers.

FAQ I WANT TO START MY OWN BUSINESS AND THINK THAT SELLING MY SOAP WOULD BE A NATURAL. DON'T YOU AGREE?

It depends. I would bet that the failure rate of small soap businesses is about the same as for any other small business. If you want to make soap and generate enough income to pay for supplies - yes, you can probably start a business. If you wish to grow your business into a $50,000 a year (or better) job; that will depend on your dedication, marketing, financing, and business sense. There are several decent books available that offer advice for starting your own business - what you need, how much cash reserve, licensing and insurance, business plan, etc.

Start with a tax number, usually obtained by writing or calling your state department of revenue. Check into zoning and similar legal restrictions on cottage industries. Decide whether you wish to incorporate, form a partnership, or form a single owner business. Think about liability insurance. Think about advertising. Think about wrapping and the cost of packaging that can run as much as the cost of ingredients. These are all part of a good business plan. Finally, think about operating at a loss for two years and whether you can afford that. Get competent financial and legal advice.

The first step, of course, is to determine just what your soap costs you. What are the raw ingredient costs now, including delivery, and what would they be at the next level up in scale? Once you determine your cost per bar (or pound or loaf), **including packaging**, then you need to determine the price per bar. It would be nice to use a formula multiplying your time by so much per hour, but the reality is that there is a market established and you will compete in and with this market. Anyway, when you have cost and price you can determine the gross margin per unit - price less cost. If you have to rent a facility to make soap or a store to sell it, that will change the picture, but for the moment, leave it as it is and go to the next step. How much per month do you want or need to make? This is up to you to decide. Let's say the answer is $2,000 per month. Divide your gross margin into $2,000 and this is the number of bars or units you will need to sell each month on average, assuming no additional overhead. The final step in this abbreviated process relates to cost of sales, which is often difficult to determine ahead of time on a unit basis. This would be extra costs to rent a place to sell your soap, or gas and maintenance on a car to visit potential clients, or extra costs for lights, water, insurance, phone, a computer presence, ads in newspapers or magazines. Add up all these costs (per month) and again divide by the gross margin. This gives you the number of extra units you have to sell each month to recover your hidden costs.

Can you do it? Or perhaps, how can you do it? Here are the basics you need to put into your business plan. Do you have enough money to build and maintain inventory? You can't just take an order and then make enough soap to fill it. You need a reasonable turnaround time and that means finished soap as well as the raw materials for replacing what you sell. You will probably need to stock at least a one-month supply (or better, a two-month supply) of soap to cover irregular order patterns. And not just today. What if your business expands? Can you do it all yourself and in the same location? Do you need employees and what will that cost and how will that effect the cost and gross margin per unit?

And what about time? Why did you go into business for yourself? To be at home with the family? To realize your personal potential? To be your own boss? Long term goals need to realistically consider the time you have that you are willing, long term, to put into the business. If it becomes apparent that time demands exceed your willingness to spend the time, you have a problem. One that perhaps can be solved by hiring employees, taking on a partner, getting the family involved in the business, too. There are many ways to handle this issue, just don't let the problem take you by surprise. Plan ahead.

And one final consideration. Okay, you like making soap. You like soap. You like having your own business. Do you like selling, bookkeeping, accounting? Not everyone is comfortable going out and selling their product to the general public. Not everyone is organized or self-disciplined enough to keep track of taxes, revenue, expenses, etc. Take the time to evaluate yourself and be sure that you are willing to deal with all phases of running your own business. If you can do all of that, I'll probably see your soap in the stores very soon.

Chapter 5
Equipment You Need to Get the Job Done

The first step in actually making soap is assembling the correct tools. Glass, plastic, and metal items used for soapmaking can be safely used for food contact as long as they are thoroughly cleaned after use. Porous items such as a wooden spoon should not be used again for food and may deteriorate over time due to the action of the lye. Soaking in vinegar after each use may help prolong the life of these items, but eventually they will start to splinter and disintegrate.

FAQ

WILL I HAVE TO BUY LOTS OF EXPENSIVE EQUIPMENT TO MAKE SOAP?

No. In fact, most "soapers" get started with common kitchen equipment. A candy thermometer, steel pot, steel or plastic spoon, heat-resistant measuring cup, and some sort of a scale are the basics. Even the molds don't have to be expensive - most plastic bins, bowls, or drawer dividers can be pressed into service.

The lye and a measuring cup with water.

The lye solution should be made in a heat-resistant glass container, such as a Pyrex® measuring cup. The volume should be large enough to accommodate both the water and the lye with room to spare. A four-cup measuring cup should suffice for a 12-ounce can of lye plus 600 to 700 cc (about 2-1/2 to three cups) of water. Over time, the glass will appear cloudy or scratched. This etching process is a normal result of contact with strong lye solutions. If the etching becomes severe, the glass may be weakened and should be replaced. Some plastics can be used, but keep in mind that the plastic has to survive almost boiling water. Most plastic or glass containers that are labeled microwave safe may be used for the lye solution.

A large pot or pan is needed for the actual soapmaking. I recommend one that can accommodate twice the volume of the total of all the liquid ingredients. The construction should preferably be of stainless steel, though a ceramic lined pot will work. Aluminum, copper, and tin are *not* suitable. Lye solutions will react with aluminum, sometimes violently, eating away the container and forming hydrogen gas as a byproduct. Hydrogen is a highly flammable, explosive gas. Remember the *Hindenberg*, the German dirigible filled with hydrogen that caught fire, burned, and crashed in New Jersey just prior to the start of World War II? Avoid aluminum, copper, and tin. Iron (like cast iron) is not always suitable either, mainly due to rust formation that will turn your soap reddish brown; cast iron is generally used for reenactment demonstrations, though, so it will definitely survive and the soap will be usable. And, although I question the overall suitability, cast iron was used in soapmaking for hundreds of years without problem. I have also seen warnings to avoid Teflon™ and other nonstick coated pots as well, probably due to the ease of marring the surface and exposing the base metal of the pot.

Use stainless steel or dishwasher-safe plastic stirring spoons, paddles, spatulas, and dippers. I use a long plastic paddle with holes in the paddle that I found in a local home brewing supply store. Hand blenders (not hand mixers) can be used with care (immerse prior to turning on, and start with a low setting). This type of blender is designed to mix drinks in a glass. They are also called stick blenders. Be sure they have no immersible parts made of aluminum. Common kitchen plastic/rubber spatulas are quite useful in getting that last bit of soap out of your pot.

Yes, electric beaters or mixers can be used, but hand held units are difficult to use without splashing; a better approach is the stand type mixer with a splash guard. Blenders can also be used if you are sure the blades are stainless steel. Using a blender does limit your batch size and you need to be sure the agitation doesn't knock the top off the blender, spraying lye and oil everywhere.

If you want to make large batches, 20 to 30 pounds at a time, visit your hardware store and get a paint mixer attachment for your drill. They will probably even have some large clamps to hold it in place while it works. Great if you are working in five-gallon or larger sizes, and the price beats the hundreds of dollars for a commercial variable speed motor and mixer shaft. Be sure, though, that it is all steel, not aluminum.

A stainless steel whisk may prove useful if you intend to add powdered ingredients during saponification. Herbs, pumice, clay, and the like are readily dispersed using a whisk. For large batches, you may want to remove a portion of the soap stock, disperse the herbs in the stock, then add this mixture back to the bulk of the soap.

Any small food mill used for grinding coffee can be used to

grind dried herbs into powder. You may wish to put this powdered material through a sieve to be sure the grind is fine enough for use.

Herbs and abrasives are finely ground in a food mill before being added to soap.

Buy a stainless steel thermometer, either a dial type or immersion type reading with a range of 30°C to 110°C or 86°F to 230°F (90°F is probably the practical lower temperature limit for cold process soap and you will only need to read temperatures as high as 230°F if you are rebatching).

You may use a wide variety of objects as molds. Ordinarily, the mold will be made of plastic or lined with plastic wrap (or butcher's or waxed paper). Plastic candy or candle molds will work nicely. One of the simplest molds is a quart-size waxed milk carton, thoroughly washed and dried. PVC pipe, usually 3" in diameter, has been used successfully, either the round or down spout shaped types. PVC pipe should be carefully sealed with plastic wrap, a flat end cap, or a (removable) wax plug. Small lengths of pipe can

even be distorted with heat and pressure to form an oval mold. The mold should either be somewhat flexible or disposable. Particularly useful molds for round and rectangular bars are those made for resin casting and found in many hobby shops. And of course, soapmaking supply companies offer specialized molds in many fanciful shapes. These individual molds are available in sizes from 2-1/2 to over four fluid ounces and are easy to fill, handle, and clean. Most new soapmakers use plastic drawer organizers as their first mold. This produces a nice loaf of soap that can be easily cut into smaller bars.

Plastic molds made for resin casting are usually available from good hobby and craft stores. You can get round and rectangular molds from 2-1/2 to four fluid ounce sizes.

A simple mold made of 3" PVC pipe from the hardware store. The end is sealed with plastic wrap which is both taped and rubber banded - you really do not want to have the plastic wrap come off before you are ready.

FAQ

CAN I USE MY COOKIE CUTTERS AND MUFFIN MOLDS FOR SOAP?

Cookie cutters can generally be used without a problem, since you are cutting finished soap with little or no lye remaining. Muffin molds can be used for melt and pour soap and probably for rebatched soap without any problems. However, if the molds are aluminum, they will be attacked by cold process soap and will discolor the surface of the soap, indicating that some of the aluminum is being eaten away. Since other alternatives are readily available, it is best to avoid all aluminum molds for cold process soap.

Three angel soaps formed using candy molds.

You'll need a place to store your soap while it ages or cures. When I was first learning to make soap at home, I used what I thought were stainless steel wire racks to store my soap during curing, since they would allow air circulation on all sides of the bars. Apparently these racks were chromed steel and probably a little worn. They left brownish wire marks on the bottom of the soap, which penetrated well into the bar. At the time, I viewed this as functionally all right, but aesthetically displeasing. In retrospect, I was probably observing examples of initial oxidation catalyzed by the iron in the rack. A similar process will occasionally form orange spots ("Dreaded Orange Spots" or DOS) on the surface of the soap during storage; this is thought to be the first stages of turning the soap rancid. Although orange spots can be avoided through use of an antioxidant such as rosemary oil extract (ROE), it is better to avoid conditions that promote oxidation.

An extreme example of "Dreaded Orange Spots" from air oxidation of the soap. This can occur with highly superfatted soap or with soap stored in hot moist conditions.

You'll also need a storage container for your finished soap. There are some quite inexpensive plastic "sweater boxes" available at specialty kitchen stores and in the kitchen department of discount stores. These boxes have lids so the essential oil won't evaporate over time and the plastic is non-reactive to or with your soap. They do, however, retain moisture so care must be taken to well cure the soap prior to storing it in this sort of box, lest the moisture migrate to the surfaces and promote rancidity. A good old-fashioned shoe box will also serve well, with the soap in layers separated by clean unprinted paper.

You'll need to measure and judge your proportions by weight, not volume. Measuring cups are not accurate enough. The best type of balance or scale to start with is an electronic balance that measures in grams or tenths of grams with a capacity of 500 to 5,000 grams. One with the ability to tare (automatically subtract the weight of your container) would be ideal. OHAUS makes a scale readable to 1 gram, priced well under $100. Food balances are also available for $40 to $80 with a capacity of ten to 20 pounds, reading to about 1/16 ounce. Remember that these scales are for your ingredients, not the finished bars, if you intend to sell the soap bars by weight. Items that are sold by weight require inspected and certified scales; this may vary somewhat from state to state and country to country, but generally speaking the requirement is universal.

One of many suitable types of digital scales. This scale has a tare function and is weighing a container of lard.

Chapter 6
Basic Ingredients

Fats, Oils, Butters, Herbs, Etc.

In general, lard and vegetable oils purchased at the grocery store should be suitable for soapmaking. Be advised that olive oil comes in several varieties and grades. Olive pomace oil is frequently used for soap since it is about 10% to 15% less costly than virgin olive oils. Pomace oil is frequently manufactured by solvent extraction of the olive pits and other residue of previous pressing. However, other pomace oils are also available and can be easily confused. If you use pomace oil, *read the fine print* and be sure the product is 100% olive derived. Inferior grades of pomace may have unacceptably high peroxide value, which can lead to rancidity in the finished soap unless a stabilizing antioxidant is added. Although any grade can probably be used, olive oil tends to have a distinctive odor, which in some grades is quite pronounced. The color and odor of the oils used will usually be present to a degree in the finished soap. If you are going to delicately scent your soap, use one of the lighter, less odorous grades of oil.

A mixture of jojoba and canola oil being weighed.

Grocery stores don't usually carry coconut oil, but you can find small quantities (about one quart) in health food stores. You might also try your local bakery or movie house (if they pop their own popcorn). If you explain your purpose, they might sell you what they buy. You are looking for what is known as white coconut oil (avoid butter flavored and colored). Some restaurant supply companies stock it. Many essential oil dealers will also handle coconut, jojoba, and soybean oils, and some may carry palm oil as well. Most companies

FAQ

WHAT'S THE DIFFERENCE BETWEEN AN OIL, FAT, ESSENTIAL OIL, AND FRAGRANCE OIL?

If you are confused by these terms, you're not alone. Most new soap-makers ask about the differences. Oils and fats are both normally bland smelling materials composed of glycerin and fatty acids, but fats come from animals while oils are from vegetable sources. Both oils and fats react with lye to form a fatty acid salt, which we just call soap, plus glycerin. Essential and fragrance oils do not form soap; they are mixtures of fragrant natural or synthetic chemicals. Essential and fragrance oils do not require any adjustment in your soap recipes unless your scent specifically says it contains some vegetable oil in addition to the fragrance material.

that specifically sell soapmaking supplies will offer all the common oils and many specialty oils as well.

LYE

You can easily (usually) find lye in a grocery or hardware store in 12- or 18-ounce cans. Avoid drain openers, which contain both lye and aluminum metal. These often come in a similar can and the aluminum metal liberates hydrogen gas when dissolved in water. (The reason for this is that most drain plugs are caused by a combination of oil or fat and hair. The lye supplies heat to melt the fat and, in combination with hydrogen and aluminum, starts a chemical reaction that breaks down hair protein, making it easier to flush down the drain.)

I have heard many people ask why I use lye to make soap - lye is so harsh and dangerous. But lye is the most convenient and cheapest alkali readily available. It is important to remember that lye is an intermediate used to make soap; it is not an ingredient in your finished soap unless you have added extra, which is normally not at all desirable. That is, you plan to have all the lye consumed by the fats and oils, leaving none behind as an ingredient. Remember this if you plan to label your soap at some point. (*Note:* Unless you make cosmetic or medical claims for your soap, you are not required by the Food and Drug Administration (FDA) to list the ingredients on the label. Examples of cosmetic claims are skin softening or moisturizing; and examples of medical claims are anti-acne or anti-dandruff.)

A 12-ounce plastic can of lye being poured into deionized water to make a lye solution.

Potassium hydroxide (caustic potash) is available from a few grocery stores (generally in the same place you find sodium hydroxide, along with the drain cleaners) and from chemical supply houses. It is usually found as 1/8" pellets (about the size of split peas) that are 85% potassium hydroxide and 15% water. Potassium hydroxide is ordinarily reserved for the formation of soft and liquid soaps, since the potassium soaps are significantly more water-soluble than the sodium soaps. Soft soaps ordinarily result when potassium hydroxide is used together with a recipe rich in liquid oils, especially if the recipe is superfatted to at least 5%.

Sodium or potassium carbonate (soda ash and potash respectively) could be used in place of lye since the process of saponification can, under certain conditions, produce free fatty acids which are almost instantly neutralized to their salts. The carbonates are harder to locate than lye and they liberate carbon dioxide when they react with acids, which should lead to the generation of foam. They are also much less reactive than lye and usually require strong heating to complete their reactions. Baking soda is generally considered to be unsuitable for saponification, being substantially less reactive; and several citations in most soapmaking literature indicate that baking soda will not saponify fats and oils. It is, however, sometimes used in rendering to remove acidic contaminants from tallow without saponifying any of the fat.

WATER

Don't forget about water. Use distilled water whenever possible, though you might want to try collecting and using rain water, which is, in theory, nature's own version of distilled water. Typically tap water is too hard and contains too much magnesium and calcium ion which produces insoluble fatty acid salts (soap scum). Bottled spring water is not necessarily any softer than tap water. A workable alternative is soft water from a water softener or reverse osmosis purifier. The soft water should be low in iron as well as magnesium and calcium, since iron salts at high pH will turn brown due to formation of iron hydroxides, a gelatinous precipitate. Formation of these iron hydroxides will also consume part of your lye solution. There are several hand-held demineralizing (water softening) units now on the market, with replaceable cartridges. These make a fully acceptable substitute for bottled water.

Tap water coming through a small hand held softener into a measuring cup. Ready for the addition of lye.

LYE SEEMS SO HARSH. IS THERE ANY WAY TO MAKE SOAP WITHOUT IT?

Part of what makes lye harsh is what enables it to react with fats and oils to form soap. Good soap, however, should have no lye remaining in it; all the lye should be consumed or used by the fats and oils, making soap. It would be misleading to see a list of soap ingredients showing lye as an ingredient, since if the soap is well made, there should be no residual lye in it. It is possible to make soap without lye, but this would ordinarily require purchasing fatty acids rather than fats and oils. Fatty acids are not widely available to home soapmakers.

Colorants

It is relatively simple to use readily available vegetable dyes to tint and color soap; however, most allergic reactions are caused either by colorants (dyes) or fragrances, natural or synthetic. Some FD&C dyes can be used to color soap but they are not all stable under the very highly alkaline conditions of soapmaking (and many rapidly fade when exposed to sunlight). As with so many other special ingredients, purchase these colorants from someone who deals extensively with soap ingredients and can tell you which dyes are stable. A single tablespoon of a suitable dye can color 50 or more pounds of soap, depending on the desired color intensity. Many suppliers offer "color tabs" or "nuggets," which are dye diluted with soap. Usage rates vary depending on the supplier, but a single tab or nugget will often color from two to six pounds of soap.

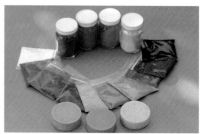

Dyes, pigments, and herbal colorants give you a wide range of color possibilities.

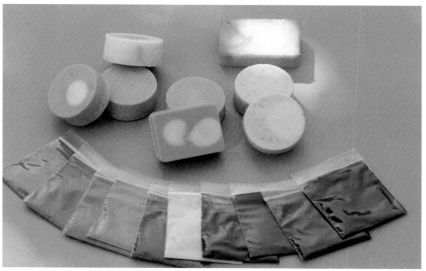

Dyes used in soapmaking.

Cosmetic grade pigments available for soapmaking.

FAQ

Can I use food coloring to color my soap?

The food coloring available in grocery stores is ordinarily considered too diluted to effectively color soap. Not all food colors are stable in soap either - the color may disappear or change to a different color altogether. Although it is not a huge defect, many dyes are not light stable, meaning they will fade if left in the sun. If you are looking for a light color tint with a small batch of soap, you might try food colors, but I would not recommend scaling up to several pounds without trying it on just a few bars first. For best results, use the dye concentrates.

Some people use aniline dyes like those used in candle making to color their soap. These dyes are much more stable than the food colors (FD&C) and are identical or closely related to the chemicals used to dye hair. In the past five to seven years, there have been concerns expressed over the toxicology of hair dyes. Although no link was demonstrated between hair dyes and various forms of cancer, I believe that discretion is the better part of valor and don't recommend the use of aniline dyes.

Pigmenting soap to produce colors is commonplace. Titanium dioxide has long been used to produce opaque, bright whites, but many beautiful pastels and vivid colors can be generated by pigments. Pigment can be either natural or synthetic. Iron oxide pigments are extensively mined in Roussillon, Provence, France, and cover a huge range of colors from yellows to reds to browns. Indian red, Turkey red, and Venetian red (covering the range from light to dark) are just a few examples of the range possible in a single color from the iron oxides. The synthetic iron oxide pigments are just industrial versions of these same naturally occurring materials, prepared from ferrous sulfate, perhaps with a tighter control of particle size. These pigments are virtually water-insoluble, stable to alkali, and colorfast in sunlight.

Of course, pigments can also be functional. Green and red clays are available which help to soften skin and can be selected to help "dry" oily skin. Pumice, mentioned elsewhere as a mild abrasive, gives a very attractive light gray appearance to the soap.

Trish, of homesong soaps, has allowed me to use this multi-layered soap as an example of the creative use of pigmented layers. Even more impressive is the fact that she created this effect in a single session to be sure the layers would stay together in use.

I strongly recommend that you request a Material Safety Data Sheet (MSDS) from any reputable supplier of chemicals and read it carefully before you put the chemical in contact with the skin for any purpose. Cosmetic grade pigments are readily available, assuring that there are no harmful levels of heavy metals or other contaminants that could prove injurious to the user. Both pigments and FD&C dyes are quite effective. A single tablespoon of pigment is often sufficient to color eight to ten pounds of soap.

Many vegetable materials are readily available for use as colorants. Annatto, turmeric, and paprika produce shades of yellow to orange. Carotene, naturally present in red palm oil and often available in gel caps in the pharmacy, produces an orange color. Red sandalwood produces a purple (at a typical use level of roughly one tablespoon per ten pounds of oil) and cocoa is sometimes used for brown, though it is also possible to get a nice medium brown by

A bar within a bar effect is created by partially filling a mold with a first color, at light trace, and then adding a thicker colored portion on top. The thicker portion resists mixing with the first color and, in use, the inner bar will be revealed as the outer layer washes away.

This is a layered soap made using a pink color tab (dye concentrate) for one layer and green in the second layer, with an optional layer of white in the middle. This bar is fresh from the freezer so note the tiny droplets of water condensing on the surface.

Cold process soap containing pumice. This soap was made in a quart milk carton but can be sliced into thinner bars.

adding herbs without an antioxidant. Chlorophyll is readily available at most pharmacies, though often in the form of gel caps, and produces a reasonable green. Green herbs, when stabilized with Vitamin E, can also be used to make green herbal bars; and I recently discovered that green kelp, from a food co-op makes a very satisfactory medium green and does not require the addition of Vitamin E stabilizer. Cochineal (derived from the shell of a beetle) is the source of many pinks to reds, though it is not especially fat-soluble, so aqueous extracts should be prepared and used. Powdered alkanet root gives a blue to bluish purple color, and is often used by steeping the powder in oil, extracting the color into the oil.

Whatever color source you choose, you can achieve interesting and often striking visual effects with the same techniques discussed in Chapter 3 in the section on rebatched soaps. Examples of two and three layer soaps and variegated imbedded soaps are shown both in Chapter 3 and Chapter 11, Soap Recipes, illustrating fun things to do with your naturally white soap.

FRAGRANCES

In general, fragrances should be added just before pouring your soap into the mold, to minimize the exposure to heat and lye. Essential oils in general offer a more intense aroma than fragrance oils and so less essential oil is usually required to scent a batch of soap. For the larger batches of soap typical with the cold process, a good starting point for fragrance addition is about one ounce (two tablespoons) for a ten pound batch of soap (made using 24 ounces of lye). For detailed information on scenting your soap, see Chapter 10.

Turmeric, cinnamon, and cocoa are often used for natural color.

FAQ

HOW CAN I MAKE A REALLY WHITE BAR OF SOAP? CAN I USE BLEACH WITH THE INGREDIENTS?

Your soap will usually be a natural white as long as you use very light vegetable oils and fats. If your ingredients are green (such as a dark olive oil or pomace) or yellow (such as some palm oils with added carotene), then your soap will be anything from a beige, a very pale green, or a yellow. If you want the soap whiter you can add titanium dioxide, a very white opaque pigment, which is commonly used in soaps. I do not recommend trying to use chlorine bleach to decolorize your oils. The chlorine can react to form chlorinated organic materials which might cause allergic skin reactions. If you really need to try bleaching your fats or oils, you could try 3% hydrogen peroxide, commonly available in most pharmacies or supermarkets. Weigh out the fats and oils in your recipe and add three to five grams of 3% hydrogen peroxide per pound of fat or oil as you start melting them together. It doesn't seem like a lot, but adding more will rarely help.

WHAT IS THE BEST WAY TO COLOR COLD PROCESS SOAP?

The answer really depends on what sort of effect you are trying to achieve. The most vivid colors usually result by adding pigment colors to the soap. Pigments make it easy to add splashes of bright color by pigmenting part of a batch and adding that in "dollops" to the mold containing uncolored soap. If you are looking for a more subdued "natural" appearance, uniform throughout the bar, then you should probably start with natural vegetable colors. Dyes are usually the best color choice for melt and pour and are very user-friendly with rebatched soap, but are a little less predictable and take a bit more cautious experimentation in cold process soap. However, if you are looking for unusual visual effects, choose a more luminous colorant.

Chapter 7
STEP-BY-STEP SOAPMAKING

Safety First

The first and most important step in soapmaking is safety. Recipes are useless unless you know and prepare for the normal hazards of production. Simply speaking, you need to protect yourself, you need to use the right pots and stirrers, and you need to protect your family and friends.

Personal protection is a necessity. You should be equipped with gloves, glasses, apron, shoes, and knowledge. Gloves protect your hands - thin close-fitting rubber gloves that do not interfere with your fingers are the best. Glasses protect your eyes from splashes, especially from lye solutions, which are highly corrosive. A simple apron protects your clothing and body. Shoes obviously protect your feet. Of course, knowledge is the hard part.

The largest safety concern focuses on the use of lye. This is a poison if taken internally and can cause very serious burns if it comes in contact with skin or eyes in solid or liquid form. It can also react with aluminum, tin, and copper, eating right through this material. In addition, dissolving solid sodium hydroxide (lye) in water generates a lot of heat - enough to boil water if the amount of water is small or if the water is warm to start. The vapors given off when sodium hydroxide is added to water are noxious, irritating and burning eyes and lungs, so operate with plenty of ventilation, preferably outdoors with the wind at your back or on the back of the stove under a strong vent. During the addition of lye to water, the temperature will increase to nearly the boiling point of water - you will see the steam. Always use room temperature water or even chilled water; warm herbal teas can boil violently if you try to dissolve lye in them without cooling.

Vinegar can be used to neutralize small lye spills. However, in case of skin or eye contact, flush the injured part with lots and lots of tepid water (under the faucet or shower) and, especially with splashes in the eyes, see a doctor right away.

If you make up your lye solution ahead of time or make extra for later use, label it and keep it away from any other containers where it might be mistaken for something else. There are terrible stories of people accidentally drinking lye and spending weeks in the hospital recovering from the internal burns. Lye should be stored in a closed container since it will absorb carbon dioxide from the air and slowly convert into sodium carbonate which will not easily saponify oils. It is a good idea to have the phone number of a poison control center posted near the phone. While you should avoid working near inquisitive children and dogs, you should not work alone in the house either. If you spill lye or set your oils on fire (they are flammable), it is good to have another pair of hands to help out. If your child or scout troop insists on a soapmaking demonstration, consider showing them melt and pour or rebatched soap.

HOW DO I PREPARE MOLDS FOR SOAPMAKING?

Molds should be very clean and dry before use. I have seen recommendations for coating the mold before use with a thin film of vegetable shortening or oil. Generally this is not necessary, but it really depends on the mold. You should also be aware that in most cases you will want to remove this material from the surface of the finished soap. A release agent is probably not necessary unless your mold is made from a porous material such as wood. Plastic molds in general do not need a release agent or aid; they just need to be clean and dry. Many people find they do not need to treat a PVC pipe mold with any release agent, while others need to spray the interior lightly with vegetable oil before filling. If you are using PVC pipe for the first time, I recommend wiping down the interior surface with olive oil just before filling. It is easier to lightly oil the mold than to fight removal of soap stuck to the surfaces.

STEP-BY-STEP INSTRUCTIONS

Assemble all the ingredients called for in the recipe you've chosen (see Chapter 11 for recipes), clean and prepare the molds (see the FAQ at left), and wear protective clothing.

Have your molds ready to go ahead of time and lay them out where you intend to fill them. Once the soap gets thick, you will not have time to clean and dry them.

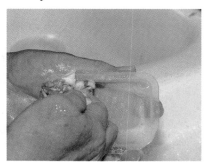

Small molds can be difficult to clean, but old soap deposits yield to dish soap, water, and elbow grease.

After selecting a recipe from Chapter 11:

1. Weigh out the appropriate amounts of fat and oil and transfer them to your soap pot.

2. Mix the fats and oils and heat to about 140°F (50°C to 60C°). Remove from the heat.

3. Measure the water and place it in the container used for the lye solution.

4. In a well ventilated area, weigh the lye and carefully pour it in the water. Mix this solution outside or on the stove top with an adequate vent fan running. When stirring, use gloves and eye protection! Remember, always add lye to water, never add water to lye. The lye solution generates enough heat to produce a final solution near the boiling point of water. Use extreme caution; I strongly suggest you wear gloves and eye protection such as glasses or goggles (not contact lenses). The final lye solution will be just under 40% lye by weight. Avoid breathing the fumes - they are very irritating to eyes and nasal passages. You might try using a painter's mask, available at most hardware stores.

Carefully stir the water as you are adding solid lye. Without stirring, it tends to form a crusty solid which is hard to safely break up, once formed.

When the lye solution turns clear, it is ready to go.

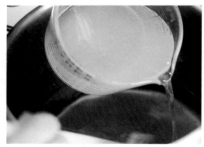

Carefully add the lye solution to the heated oils, but take care to avoid splashing.

As the reaction proceeds, the soap thickens visibly. You will be able to feel the difference as well as see it.

5. When the lye is completely dissolved and the solution is clear, stir it into the warm oil. This can be done fairly rapidly, taking care to avoid splashing. Very soon the oil will become murky from the soap crystals that are forming. Keep stirring and the oil will become opaque and finally thicken into a custard-like consistency. The soap is ready to scent or mold when the oil and lye phases no longer separate and you can form a "trace" on the surface (see the FAQ at right). Although the time for this is ordinarily about 30 minutes, it can take as long as four hours with ordinary stirring, depending on conditions. If it is not thickening, check the temperature. If the temperature has dropped below 100°F, gently reheat the pot on the stove to about 120°F. If you have a stick blender available, several ten to 20 second pulses usually serve to thicken the batch.

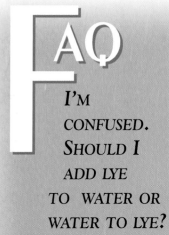

FAQ

I'M CONFUSED. SHOULD I ADD LYE TO WATER OR WATER TO LYE?

The safest way is to always add lye to water. Although it is sometimes considered easier to weigh lye by adding it into a container of water, this is not a safe practice due to the amount of heat liberated when mixing lye and water.

FAQ

WHAT DOES "TRACE" MEAN?

*I use the common term "tracing," which is a sign that the soap mixture has become a stable emulsion and is ready to pour into molds. The solution traces if, when you take a spoonful out of the pot and pour it back in, you can see a faint impression remaining briefly on the surface of the liquid where the liquid went in. Those of you who are proficient cooks can, with a little practice, determine visually when a stable emulsion has formed. If you get confused about trace, think **thick but pourable**. The soap should not readily settle into layers when you stop stirring it.*

6. When the soap is thickened, add fragrance, herbs, colorants, etc. with good agitation. You may want to use a stainless steel whisk to disperse solids such as clay, ground oatmeal, ground herbs, or pigments.

Add essential oils by the spoonful.

7. Pour the thickened soap into molds. Leave the molds in a warm place (70°F to 80°F) for one to two days. This allows the saponification reaction to continue until complete and the bars will harden enough to maintain their shape.

A ladle is a handy tool for transferring the soap mixture into your molds.

Recently filled molds; still quite liquid.

Once in the mold, your soap will usually appear solid within a few hours. It is still very soft at this point.

8. Freeze the mold for three to eight hours or overnight. Soap in plastic molds can be removed by heating the bottom in hot tap water for several seconds. PVC pipe molds may take a little longer and a hair dryer may be a better choice to gently heat the exterior of this mold. Invert and gently push on the bottom to release the soap. If you need to push hard on the soap to extricate it from the mold, place the metal top of an orange juice can against the surface of the soap and push against it with a thick wooden dowel. Metal molds can also be heated with a hair dryer and the soap pushed out. Cut or tear off paper molds. Cut the soap to size if necessary. A

thin wire such as a cheese cutter, clay slicer, guitar string, or piano wire works if you can keep it taut. For the person intent on scaling up, a jig saw or band saw will also work (use a blade designed to cut plastic).

Dip the bottom of the mold in warm water for five to ten seconds to loosen the soap.

Once the soap is loose, push the bottom and flex the mold like an ice cube tray to pop the soap out.

Once the soap breaks free from the mold, it will slip out.

9. Rest the soap on waxed or butcher's paper until it is firm enough so your touch doesn't cause an indentation, usually one or two days. Move the soap to storage but allow for plenty of air circulation around the bars. After about two to four weeks, examine the soap for light(er) surfaces. This could indicate the presence of sodium carbonate, formed when unreacted lye comes into contact with carbon dioxide from the air. This material should be scraped off and discarded or, better yet, saved for the laundry.

10. Cured soap can then be wrapped and/or placed in storage. Cardboard shoe boxes, plastic sweater boxes, plastic wrap, etc. are all suitable for storage.

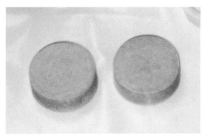

By freezing the soap and mold, the resulting bar is usually quite smooth and even.

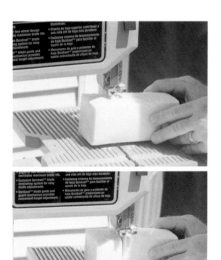

Here I am cutting pumice soap made using paper milk cartons as molds into slices. The speed of the band saw usually eliminates the tendency of soap to crumble and the blade is sharp enough to easily penetrate fully cured soap.

Now the hard work is done. Released from the mold, the soap is ready to be cured and dry out for 3 to 5 weeks.

FAQ

WHAT'S THAT WHITE STUFF ON THE SURFACE OF MY SOAP?

The composition of a white surface layer, usually called ash, that sometimes occurs on soap is a matter of debate. Soap actually can exist in any of four interchangeable crystalline forms. Which type of crystal forms depends on a variety of factors such as the temperature where the crystals form and the amount of water in the mix. The physical description of one particular form, designated as the "beta" form, seems to match the physical properties of what we usually call "ash." At least one soapmaker has had her ash layer analyzed by an outside laboratory and only soap was found. This supports the likelihood that most ash is really just another form of soap crystal. The often expressed observation that rebatched or Castile (100% olive oil) soap bars have a different texture also indicates (at least to me) that we often create these different crystal structures (called polymorphs if you must know) without realizing it. The term ash rightly refers to sodium carbonate which can form from exposure of excess lye (in soap) to the air.

CLEANING UP

Sooner or later it happens to the best of us. You have your soap in molds and a stack of dirty pots and utensils in the sink. What now? First of all, that is not yet soap covering all those surfaces. The pH is still very high, it can still cause burns, and it will laugh at water. In fact, it will coat everything it touches with an oily layer. You might want to wait overnight to let chemistry complete the soap transformation. It will be easier to clean then. If you have a septic tank, I strongly suggest you scrape as much residual soap as possible out of the pot and off the utensils and put the scrapings in the garbage. You don't want to damage your septic field or plug up the drains. If you need to clean up right away, keep your gloves on.

You can use a little vinegar to cut the pH to a safer level and scrub with a lot of soap or detergent and a brush, rinsing several times along the way to remove oily water. You can also put the items in the dishwasher, since dishwasher detergent is very high in alkali (so high that dishwashers can't have aluminum parts exposed). If you do use the dishwasher, run everything through a second time.

Dirty pots and utensils are most easily cleaned after 24 hours, when the oils have mostly converted into soap. Fresh soap is quite oily and hard to clean.

TROUBLESHOOTING

Here are a few of the most common problems encountered with cold process soapmaking.

1. My soap won't trace. What can I do?

This usually happens when making nearly 100% olive oil soaps, which can take hours (and sometimes days) to trace. Maintain a reasonable temperature and agitate the mixture periodically. It will slowly solidify. If you aren't making a high olive oil soap, check your ingredients to be sure you added the correct amount of lye. Insufficient lye is another possible cause.

2. The soap traced but turned to liquid once I put it in the mold.

This is probably an example of

a false trace. False trace usually happens when the reaction temperature drops low enough to let the solid fats or oils solidify before they saponify. Put the mixture back in the soap pot and reheat while stirring until it traces again. Next time you make this soap, check your starting temperatures.

3. The soap traced but once it was placed in the mold, a thin oily layer formed on top.

This is probably your essential or fragrance oil separating out. It will normally be re-absorbed into the soap, so just wait a day or so.

4. The top of the soap turned into a white powder.

The white powder is probably ash. The most common solution is to scrape it off. Next time try covering the exposed surface of the soap (in the mold) with plastic wrap.

5. During (or after) curing, I noticed brown or orange spots on the surface of the soap.

Those dreaded orange spots are usually from oxidation of excess oils. Reduce your superfat level or add an antioxidant to the soap during saponification.

6. When I was taking my soap out of the molds, I noticed a liquid layer at the bottom.

This layer, usually brownish, is generally caused when the lye solution separates from the soap. Check your weights to be sure you didn't add too much lye (or too little oil). It is best to discard the entire soap batch when this happens.

7. I was just about to pour my soap into the mold when I remembered that I had forgotten to add one of the oils in the recipe.

The soap is now lye heavy. You can either try to reheat the soap gently (to make it more liquid) and add the forgotten oil, or you could try rebatching it with the addition of the forgotten oil.

8. I tried to use my cured soap, but it was white and crumbly instead of nicely solid.

Be careful and check your ingredients. This could be an indication of too much lye. The other possibility is that you used too much solid fat or oil, which sometimes causes the soap to crack or become crumbly. A good soap is usually a balance of solid and liquid fats or oils.

9. My soap is good but the fragrance disappeared after only a few weeks.

Some fragrances are unstable or too volatile for soapmaking. Try a small batch with twice the amount of fragrance and see if that lasts. If not, you have just found a fragrance that is not suitable for use in cold process soapmaking. You might try rebatching the non-fragrant soap and adding the fragrance oil. If it is unstable to highly alkaline conditions, it is likely to be more stable to rebatching.

10. Everything was doing fine until I added the fragrance oil at trace and the soap suddenly seemed to heat up and get solid very quickly.

You have found a fragrance oil that causes seizing. In the future, if you must use this oil, add it much earlier, at very thin trace, and be prepared to quickly put the soap in molds if it still seems to thicken too much.

11. I made some soap for gifts and now all my friends want to buy some to give as gifts.

This is not considered a problem. You friends have just discovered what you already know - the wonderful properties of hand-made, hand-crafted soap. Congratulations.

CHAPTER 8
SIX SOAPMAKING SECRETS

There are few true secrets to making good soap, though this is not always obvious to the novice. There are, of course, shortcuts and rules of thumb that help a beginner gain confidence and become proficient at the many aspects of this craft.

SECRET #1 - PATIENCE

The first, biggest, and most underrated secret is patience. I have never had a pot of "ingredients" not make soap, even if it did not quite resemble what I had in mind originally. Let me repeat that. If my recipe had the correct amount of lye and oil, I have always been able to produce good soap. This appears to be one distinct advantage of making soap at elevated starting temperatures.

When making my first several batches, I expected to finish in an hour or so, and it did not happen that way. Then I came to expect four-hour batches. Later I found that I could adjust (shorten) the time required by making slight changes in the formula - starting out at a slightly higher temperature, changing the rate of mixing, or reheating the pot when it cools off. I even poured batches into molds when the "brew" seemed nowhere near thick enough. Basically, if your proportions are correct, you can pour soap into a mold as long as it pours and the oil does not separate into a separate layer on top when it stands without stirring.

And if it does separate? Wait. Have patience. Wait as long as a week or two if needed. Stir it in the mold if that is possible. I have never had to throw away a batch of soap. Sometimes that thin top layer of oil is actually your fragrance oil separating out just a bit. When that happens, be assured that it will be drawn back into the soap as it solidifies. However, if you pour off the top liquid oily layer, your proportions are no longer correct and you will be left with a large excess of lye and no way to correct it with certainty.

SECRET #2 - INS CALCULATION

The second very important secret, not widely known, is the use of an artificial calculation called **INS** to evaluate the ratio of oils in your recipe. Although I do not know what caused the original scientist to call this term "INS," it is just possible that this term reflects its relationship to its origins, since it is calculated from the Iodine Value and Saponification Value. I(odine value) 'n S(ap value.) Whatever its derivation, to save you time and trouble, I have included the INS value in my table of oils on page 116. The INS value for a mixture of oils is simply the weighted average INS value for the mixture of oils. Most importantly, the source indicated that they had determined that the "ideal" INS average value for a fat or oil mixture for a bar of toilet soap is around 160.

That innocent discovery set the wheels in motion and a quick scrutiny of my own recipes showed an INS nearly in the optimum range. Further calculations of many published recipes were also either in or close to the ideal range. Needless to say, I adjusted my recipes and ingredients to get closer to this range. As I have said, you can make soap from almost any mixture of fats and oils, but if you want to experiment, try the INS calculation before you make your soap and see how close you are.

The INS for cottonseed oil is listed as 88. The INS for coconut oil is about 257 and olive oil is about 107, while palm is 206. You can then calculate that in a blend of 25% coconut, 25% cottonseed, 25% olive, and 25% palm oils, the INS factor is 164.5 ([88 + 257 +107 + 206] ÷ 4), confirming that this mixture would make a near ideal soap as far as hardness and other physical properties are concerned. This would be an excellent starting point for a soap containing cottonseed oil.

SECRET #3 - TEMPERATURE AND AGITATION

The third secret is that the speed of saponification (how fast oil converts to soap) is dependent both on temperature and agitation. The reaction itself is exothermic, which means that heat is produced as the reaction proceeds and also that the right mixture of ingredients really "want" to make soap. However, since oil and water do not mix, the only reaction that can take place is at the small layer where the lye solution comes into contact with the oil. Even though higher temperatures speed up the reaction, at least in the beginning, higher temperatures cause the oil and water to have less contact. To counteract this, increase agitation. For very small batches, the blender is quite efficient; you can go from a two-phase liquid system to solid soap almost before you know it. For batches up to ten or so pounds, the stick blender is one way to speed up the process. After the lye solution is stirred into the oil for about five minutes, the stick blender can be used in cycles of 30 seconds on, 60 seconds off (to avoid overheating the blender) until

Most soapmakers like to have a stick blender, like the one shown, handy to encourage reluctant soap reactions to thicken.

trace is reached, usually within five to ten minutes. After that, continue with regular stirring and add other ingredients as desired.

Is the stick blender a solution to all worries? No. The difficulty comes when this blender is used with blends rich in hard oils, such as palm or vegetable shortening, at low temperatures, usually around 90°F. It is possible to form a thick emulsion of oil and lye solution, rather like mayonnaise, that appears to be ready to pour into a mold. However, if the actual chemical reaction is too incomplete, saponification will proceed in the mold, generating heat as it goes. And this heat can cause two adverse reactions. The smaller problem is that the heat can actually melt the center of the soap in the mold, so the result will appear to be a dark, sometimes almost transparent center with normal looking soap surrounding it. Both the center and edges will usually be good quality soap, quite usable, but may not look as you intended. The more serious problem is that as the soap heats up, it might separate into oil and lye solution phases which will cause the formation of pockets of lye in the finished soap. Soap with lye pockets or layers is not safe to be used.

In most cases a careful visual inspection will alert you to problems. If the soap does not get firm, it is probably under-reacted; it never got hot enough for saponification to complete. Perhaps rebatching can save this soap.

If the soap has that dark, almost translucent center, cut a bar open and examine the center. Good soap should be a nice uniform color and consistency. Pockets or layers of white, usually crumbly material, could very easily be lye. Check the pH (using pH indicator papers available from most swimming pool supply shops) to see if it is unusually high; lye will ordinarily give you a reading at or near 14 - extremely caustic. Check your recipe again to be sure that your calculations were correct and the proper amount of lye and oil were used. If the proportions were correct, rebatching might well salvage this batch too.

Of course, the best thing is simply to avoid the problem in the first place. Check the temperature while you are stirring the oil and lye. If the temperature drops below 100°F before the batch thickens or traces, it might be desirable to gently and carefully heat slightly to encourage saponification. If you have made this recipe before and this batch behaves significantly different than the last one, check your ingredient proportions and temperatures carefully and you will usually avoid problems.

SECRET #4 - SALVAGING A BATCH IN JEOPARDY

The fourth secret lies in accepting that sometimes your best laid plans will go wrong at the last minute and planning ahead to salvage the batch. When you add essential oil, aloe vera gel, or herbs and other finely ground material to a warm soap batch ready to pour, these ingredients - which will be much cooler than the soap mixture - may cause a sudden large rise in viscosity. One definite reason is that viscosity tends to rise with falling temperature. For example, gravy is thicker cold than hot. A second possible cause is due to shock crystallization. Any number of things, such as a sudden change in concentration, a sudden change in temperature, or a sudden addition of high surface area solids, can cause this phenomenon, which is essentially the abrupt formation of mega-scads (that's the technical term) of extremely small soap crystals (sometimes referred to as crystallites). These small crystals rub together and cause the dramatic increase in viscosity. Is this a problem? Only if the mixture gets too thick to pour into a mold - and it can. You could be stuck with a pot of soap and no way to get it out except to scoop it out and make soap balls.

When soap reaches this stage, with a consistency similar to applesauce, it is unwise to add anything that would tend to make it thicker.

As you can see by the standing "squiggle" on the top, this soap has, or has very nearly, seized.

As your soapmaking skill increases, you will learn to recognize the warning signs of impending complications. For example, you'll recognize when the mixture has thickened to the point of tracing and is still hot. It is good to have alternative plans ready to implement. Such as? Change your plans, omit the powdered oatmeal and herbs and add only essential oils to the mix-

ture and quickly get your molds ready. Another possible change is to forget about the small fancy molds you were going to use and grab the clean dry quart milk cartons you have been saving for just this sort of impending disaster. Spoon the thickened soap mixture in if it won't pour and settle it by pinching the top closed and thumping it repeatedly on the table. As another alternative, try making that rebatched soap or maybe make bars by using the hydraulic mold your spouse put together for you. In this case, let the soap solidify in manageable chunks, grate or chop it and use the result in your endeavors. Crossing your fingers or saying a prayer might help, but adding water usually does not.

But what happens if you get your soap started and the phone rings? Or if it takes longer than planned and dinner is served? It doesn't matter what happens to cause an interruption - eventually it will happen. If it happens early in the soapmaking process, don't worry. The oil and lye solution will separate and the reaction will virtually come to a stop except at the interface - that thin space where water and oil are in contact. During this time, the soap crystals will normally settle to the bottom of the pot. They often feel sort of grainy, like large granules, when you stir them up again. So stir them up thoroughly, reheat the pot a little if it has cooled to room temperature, and go on.

There are, of course, potential disasters that are not so easily remedied. What happens when you are looking with pride at the solidifying soap you have just put into your mold and you realize you forgot to add 25% of the oils required? If your batch is still in the pot and has not reached that firm trace stage, you should be able to add the additional oils, though it would help if you could warm the forgotten oils first and then dribble them in with slow continuous stirring. The risk is that cold oil may cause shock crystallization by dropping the batch temperature, essentially seizing the batch. In any event, rewarming should be possible but potentially tricky. In some cases it may be simpler just to let the soap set overnight, carefully grate it (realizing that it will be *very* lye heavy) and then rebatch it with the missing oils as part of the rebatch.

SECRET #5 - IT'S NOT SET IN STONE

The fifth secret is that there is no universally right set of conditions to use in soapmaking. The temperature of the lye solution does not have to match the temperature of the oils. There is no single best temperature to start with. When you make the exact same recipe many times, the time to trace can vary greatly. The common thread here is uncontrolled temperature variables. High temperatures (oils at 140°F, lye solution at 160°F) are very suitable for filling small or individual molds, which rapidly lose heat once they are filled so you need to compensate for the heat loss. For the same reason, even though the initial temperatures are the same, a ten pound batch will get to trace faster than a five pound batch in the same pot. Larger volumes retain more heat. Similarly, with a cluster of small molds, those in the center will remain warmer than those on the ends - and as a result, the center molds will become solid faster than those on the end.

An array of molds filled with oatmeal honey soap.

Gently press the soap surface to see if it is firm enough to remove from the mold.

Large flat molds will generally require using a lower temperature than small molds since the retained heat in the center could actually cause melting and discoloration. Temperatures around 130°F to 140°F are more appropriate for flat molds, which should ordinarily not be insulated for the first few hours after filling. Shoe box or cubic molds will probably require starting temperatures in the range of 120°F to 130°F and rarely need to be insulated at all.

SECRET #6 - FRAGRANCE CONCERNS

Fragrances should be added near the end of soapmaking, just before putting the soap into the mold. As your expertise increases, you should learn, at least in general, the chemical components of the fragrance you want to use. Most fragrance chemicals fall into one of the following chemical types: alcohols, aldehydes, ketones, esters, and olefins. Chemical names don't have to be daunting and you don't have to memorize a long list of names. Look at the endings of the chemical names. Alcohols, such as the common fragrance alcohol linalool, usually end in "ol," while aldehydes usually end in "al" or even aldehyde (no one ever said chemists had to be consistent). Olefins, which are unsaturated hydrocarbons, are among the most stable fragrance compounds and usually end in "ene," as in cedrene or limonene. Esters usually have two names, reflecting the alcohol and acid they came from (i.e. methyl laurate is the name of an ester).

Aldehydes and esters are common fragrance components that are unstable to basic conditions. That is, aldehydes and esters, if used to fragrance soaps, can be expected to either lose much of their aroma or change the type of aroma they generate. It is very challenging to produce a stable citrus aroma of any sort since citral, the primary essence of most citrus oils, is an aldehyde and unstable to alkali and limonene, another major fragrance chemical component, is easily air oxidized. Benzaldehyde is the main fragrance chemical in almond extract (or synthetic almond fragrance) and maraschino cherry aroma. Benzaldehyde, obviously an aldehyde based on its name, would definitely undergo reactions if added too early in the soapmaking process, though it is more stable than most aldehydes. Ketones and olefins are much more stable, but even so, they should be added just before pouring the soap into molds.

Fragrance oils should be purchased from a reputable dealer who understands soapmaking, since many fragrance oils (as well as a few essential oils such as cinnamon, clove, allspice, and nutmeg) will accelerate saponification to the point that the entire batch can seize - thicken and turn to something similar to cottage cheese or worse - in a matter of seconds. Although several factors can cause your cold process soap to seize, essential oils that contain significant amounts of the natural chemical compound eugenol should definitely be used with caution. (*Note:* Cinnamon, nutmeg, allspice, and clove essential oils all contain high levels of eugenol.) My belief is that eugenol acts as a catalyst for saponification, greatly accelerating the rate of reaction. I vividly remember one demonstration where I added cinnamon essential oil to soap contained in several milk carton molds. (I added it in the mold since I knew that this oil could cause the soap to seize. I thought I was being smart.) As I was setting up for my next demonstration, an unfamiliar sound made me look at the soap I had just made. It was now steaming and beginning to foam up and out of the mold. Disaster? No, all I did was separate the soap molds and let them cool down, which eliminated the foaming.

CHAPTER 9
ADDITIVES TO CUSTOMIZE SOAP

Soaps are ordinarily designed to contain a wide variety of additives, color and fragrance being the most common. **Essential oils** *- pressed, extracted, or distilled from various plants - are most often used since they tend to be relatively stable during the highly alkaline soapmaking process. Essential oils from herbs also have various therapeutic benefits associated with them.* **Fragrance oils** *are fragrances that are synthetic, though many of their components may be natural, and are blends formulated to emulate a natural fragrance (such as raspberry or lilac).* **Dried herbs,** *generally ground to a powder, can also be used. They can produce a variety of colors and can contribute some fragrance to the soap, though their aroma is much less pronounced than their corresponding essential oils.*

Many easy-to-grow herbs, such as Echinacea, can be added to your soap when they are dried and ground to a powder or made into a tea.

There is quite a bit of debate about whether essential oils maintain their healthful properties when used in soapmaking. Heat during saponification, contact with strong alkali, and short contact time during washing are all cited as reasons to doubt the benefit of using essential oils. Direct evidence is typically lacking, though apocryphal accounts abound. Finally, a majority of aromatherapy practitioners agree that essential oils in soap do have at least some, if not all, of their healthful properties if the soap is produced under conditions where the aroma retains the character of the original oil. Even with brief skin contact, it is certainly better to apply a therapeutic essential oil than not; and in any event, inhalation (of the fragrance, not the soap) is certainly the easiest mechanism to introduce essential oils into the body by exchange in

An electric food mill, shown here with a mixture of chamomile and ground oatmeal, is very useful for powdering and mixing herbs and coarse pigments before adding them to soap.

the nasal mucous membrane. I personally believe in the use of essential oils because I have seen many lingering skin conditions helped by use of soap containing the appropriate essential oils.

ABRASIVES are also fairly common in hand soaps, since they help scour or loosen dirt from nooks and crannies (e.g. under fingernails). Pumice, a porous volcanic rock, can be used as well as a variety of organic materials such as finely ground oatmeal, cornmeal, and nut meal and hulls. Abrasiveness increases roughly in this order: oatmeal, cornmeal, nut meal, nut hulls, pumice. Mild abrasives also function to exfoliate the skin - help slough off old dry skin cells, exposing the softer underlayer. In practical terms for home soapmaking, one to two cups of abrasive are sufficient in a ten pound batch of soap.

Mild abrasives commonly found in your kitchen include (clockwise from top), coffee grounds, corn meal, nut meats, and oatmeal.

If excess oil (or fatty acid) is added to the soap (more than can react with the lye provided), the soap is termed SUPERFATTED. In actuality, unreacted fat or oil is unlikely to remain completely unchanged during soapmaking, since there is an excess of water and glycerin available with which to react. The excess oil most likely transforms into a complex mixture of semi-reacted materials such as fatty acids and glycerides. These com-

pounds are well known EMOLLIENTS - skin softeners and moisturizers that can actually be absorbed into the outer layers of the skin and fortunately don't necessarily leave an oily residue on the skin. A wide range of materials are used commercially today in soap and detergent bars. The simplest, of course, are either excess oil or excess fatty acids. Mineral oil, lanolin, and fatty alcohols have often been used, but today are of questionable value due to the possibility of clogging skin pores and potentially promoting acne.

For the home soapmaker, superfatting is usually accomplished by either reducing the calculated lye requirement by a fixed amount (a "lye discount") or by adding extra oil, usually at trace or during a rebatching step. Often, more expensive oils and vegetable butters are added this way so that saponification is kept to a minimum. Levels of superfatting normally range from 1% to 15%, but levels above 7% usually require the addition of an antioxidant to help stabilize and preserve the soap from spoiling. A more desirable range for superfatting is an excess of 3% to 5%, which ordinarily does not require antioxidants unless the soap is made and stored in a warm moist climate (Hawaii, Florida, etc.).

Other emollients are naturally occurring components of vegetable oils, especially olive oil, which are chemically unrelated to the oils themselves. These unsaponifiable materials have a variety of chemical forms and are present in quantities from hardly measurable up to 11% of the total oil. Although any oil can be used to superfat soap, more expensive, skin beneficial oils should be added at trace or during rebatching to preserve the properties of the oil,

HOW DO I ADD SILK TO MY SOAP?

To achieve a truly "silky" feeling soap, you can actually add silk to your soap. The easiest way to add silk protein is to add a few small pieces of silk to the lye solution right after it is mixed. Although you may have to push the silk down in the lye solution with a spoon until it gets thoroughly wet, it should dissolve fairly readily. Then just use this solution to make your soap.

which are often lost by saponification. The principal role of these natural emollients in soap and cosmetics, however, is as an occlusive agent - a fatty material deposited on the skin to retard moisture loss and keep the skin from drying out.

PROTEIN is often added for skin and hair softening. There are several natural sources of protein available to the home soapmaker, the simplest being milk. Cleopatra reportedly bathed in milk (goat, mare, or ass, depending on the story you hear) for her fabled complexion. Today, goat milk is usually available in most parts of the country and powdered goat's milk is available at most health food stores. It is also possible to dissolve silk, a natural protein material, in lye and use this in your soapmaking. Oatmeal, previously mentioned as a mild abrasive, also imparts a soft smooth character to the skin.

Other additives used are HUMECTANTS (honey, propylene glycol, or glycerin) which are also skin moisturizers, LUBRICANTS (such as bentonite and other clays used in shaving soaps to provide a thin layer of small platelets to protect the skin as the blade glides across the surface), and ANTIOXIDANTS and STABILIZERS (such as Vitamins A, C, or E or certain herbal extracts such as rosemary oil extract,

ROE). Certain other raw materials, such as jojoba oil, have both fatty acid and fatty alcohol content, providing high levels of soap together with emollient action from the fatty alcohol. (Jojoba oil has the added benefit of rarely spoiling.)

Mass-produced soap generally has the natural glycerin removed and so lacks this natural moisturizer which cold processed soap retains. Glycerin also tends to boost foaming and so is sometimes added back to a complexion bar to overcome the lather suppressing effect of adding the extra fat. Again, in cold process soap that is superfatted, retained glycerin is the reason we can produce a mild soap with good or superior foaming properties. It is even possible and often desirable to add extra glycerin to formulations for shaving soap that benefit from a longer lasting stable foam.

And, of course, many commercial soap bars are composed either partially or totally of synthetic detergents. Those without soap are generally called syndets for synthetic detergent. Dove, a leading complexion bar, is reported to be roughly 26% stearic acid and 55% synthetic detergent, Igepon A, while Zest is reportedly a combar (combination of synthetic detergent and soap, in this case a blend of two synthetic detergents, glycerol ether sulfonate, fatty alcohol sulfate, and soap).

CHAPTER 10
CREATING FRAGRANCE - WRITING A SOAP OPERA

No matter what type of soap you make, the odds are that you want to give it a fragrance that is as wonderful as its visual appeal. Fragrance creation is like writing an opera. Each fragrance component has a characteristic note and when notes are combined and balanced, the result is a full, round fragrance. For soapmakers, the units of fragrance that contain the notes are usually selected from essential oils, fragrance oils, and herbs (or infusions).

FRAGRANCE FROM ESSENTIAL OILS

Essential oils are usually isolated from the flowers, leaves, or roots of a plant by steam distillation. The appropriate part of the herb is placed in or above water in a boiler and this floral mix is boiled, often under reduced pressure. The steam is collected and condensed and the insoluble essential oils rise to the top and are removed. The fragrant water condensate left behind is termed a floral water such as rose water or lavender water. Essential oils are highly concentrated and are usually not suitable to use directly on the skin because of their concentrated nature. The yield of essential oil varies with the plant, but often only a few pounds of oil are obtained from hundreds of pounds of plant. They are usually priced accordingly, but frequently only a

teaspoon or two are needed to scent a kilogram (2.2 pounds) of soap.

The true benefit of essential oils is their historical medicinal use in aromatherapy, which proposes that herbal fragrance can stimulate the brain to affect mental states and physical well being. There is quite a bit of literature available dealing with the use of specific essential oils to calm,

Bags of rose petals fresh from the Turkish fields are ready to be fed into the still in the background. Photo by Butch Owen.

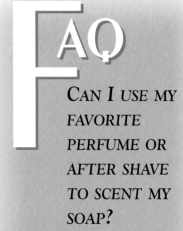

FAQ

CAN I USE MY FAVORITE PERFUME OR AFTER SHAVE TO SCENT MY SOAP?

You might be able to do it, but since both types of scent have a fairly high alcohol content, you may run the risk of seizing your soap before you add enough to give your soap an appreciable fragrance.

reduce depression or stress, or even stimulate the immune system. Some essential oils, such as lavender, are also quite good for the skin and are widely used, diluted in a carrier (vegetable) oil, in massage therapy.

Although there has been some debate as to the level of benefit derived from using essential oils in soap, the consensus seems to be that if the scent remains true, there should be at least some benefit when it's used in soap, in addition to providing a totally natural fragrance. And, since not all fragrance is washed away with the lather, there should be some residual benefit to the skin. Of course, caution is needed in selecting essential oils for soap, since not all are recommended for skin contact. See the list starting on page 68 for the benefits and effects of different essential oils, including warnings against the use of some commonly available essential oils.

FRAGRANCE FROM FRAGRANCE OILS

You can readily find oils in various hobby and craft stores labeled as fragrance oils. These will not always give satisfactory results unless they are intended for use in soapmaking. Fragrance oils designed specifically for soapmaking are available by mail order from a number of suppliers (see Resources on page 120). Vendors should be able to tell you if there is any adverse effect on your soapmaking process, such as causing

cold process soap to seize (see Chapter 2, Glossary). The highest quality fragrance oils are often a blend of natural and synthetic components and may contain as many as 30 separate components. Originally, fragrance oils were compounded by expert perfumers, relying on their trained noses and experience with fragrance components. Today, many fragrances are duplicated by using complex modern instrumentation to separate and identify volatile fragrance components and then blending known components to duplicate the fragrance profile.

It is not correct to state broadly that no therapeutic benefit can be obtained from a fragrance oil. Since the content of these oils are trade secrets, it is also impossible to say that there *are* any benefits in using them. The big advantage, of course, is that fragrance oils offer a wide range of affordable fragrances, especially those that are not available as essential oils or those that are available but prohibitively expensive. Perfumers tend to use natural and synthetic fragrances together, looking for a final wondrous effect, unconcerned with trying to label their product "natural." And there is certainly nothing wrong with that.

FRAGRANCE FROM EXTRACTS

It is also possible to use extracts such as vanilla, lemon, or almond. There is nothing wrong with trying, but these extracts are not overly strong smelling. If you need to add a lot to get the desired fragrance level, consider using an essential oil. If that option is not available to you, try writing or phoning the extract maker. Often more concentrated extracts designed for professional bakers and food formulators are available. These are not sold at the grocery store, so you need to contact the extract maker directly. You may also be able to purchase extracts from a local bakery if you explain what you are doing. You do need to consider that most extracts contain at least some alcohol. Too much alcohol can lead to instability in the soap mixture, leading to either oil/water separation or seizing, so start on a small scale and be cautious. I have repeatedly had success using concentrated lemon extracts (together with powdered lemon peel and lemongrass) but have been unable to generate a lasting vanilla aroma using its extract.

FRAGRANCE FROM HERBS

In general, herbs should be dried and ground for use in soap, though occasionally herbal teas are used to replace some or all of the water for the lye solution. If you want to avoid darkening of the herbs, incorporate an antioxidant such as Vitamin E into your soap. Be aware that Vitamin E can be purchased as a pure oil as well as in a vegetable oil carrier such as sesame oil. Vitamin E from "natural" sources such as wheat germ oil can also be used. Vitamin C, another readily available antioxidant, is itself an acid and additional lye should be used to neutralize the

acid groups if this is used. Some herbs contain natural antioxidants and do not require additional ingredients. Lavender, of course, is the most commonly used herb in soapmaking, but rosemary, sage, chamomile, hops, lemongrass, and many other beneficial herbs are used to enhance the visual and aromatic appeal and skin soothing properties of soap.

FRAGRANCE FROM INFUSED OILS

If you have a fragrant garden, it is also possible to make your own infused oils. Here, flowers are covered with oil and either gently heated for an hour or two in the top of a double boiler or left to warm in the sun for 24 to 48 hours. The soaked flowers can then be removed and new flowers added to intensify the fragrance transferred to the oil. Infused oils can be used either as a base oil or added at trace or during rebatch to fragrantly superfat the soap.

Linden blossoms are pressed to the bottom of a glass container.

Jojoba or olive oil is added to completely cover the blossoms.

The container is covered to keep it free from insects and allowed to sit in the sun.

The infused oil is filtered and can be stored or used again with more blossoms to increase the intensity of the scent.

MAKING THE FRAGRANCE DECISION

When it comes to selecting a fragrance for your soap, there are three distinctly different approaches.

1. You can select a single essential or fragrance oil because you like the scent or want the specific healing properties of the essential oil.

2. You can blend two or three essential oils into your soap, based on the reported aromatherapy properties of the oils. Blends with beneficial effects greater than individual oils are called synergies. You can choose oils that are uplifting or healing, have a physical effect or an emotional or psychic one. It is generally counterproductive to blend oils with opposing effects, such as calming and invigorating, but you might use lavender essential oil, which is relaxing, with rosemary essential oil, which is energizing, because lavender can also be stimulating since it reduces stress and anxiety.

Once you have selected a number of potential oils to use for scent, you need to blend them harmoniously - the right amount of each oil. A good way to blend oils based on their fragrance rather than therapeutic characteristics, is described below. Remember, you have already selected the oils for their therapeutic benefit, now you want to fine tune the fragrances. There is at least one theory that says that if a specific aroma really turns you off, you don't need the oil - your body is telling you something.

3. Finally, you can blend fragrances for perfumery effect alone. The soap industry giants pay a lot of money to develop a fragrance that is widely attractive and distinctive. You can do this yourself, using essential oils, fragrance oils, or combinations of both. Since it would be rather costly to make up a batch of soap every time you wanted to try out a new fragrance combination, try this: Place a differently scented drop of oil on one of several cotton swabs. Then bundle swabs with different fragrances in a plastic bag and test their fragrance; then try a different grouping of swabs. Of course, the final fragrance will be subtly different when the scents are actually blended together, but you can make an excellent approximation.

Cotton swabs, dipped in essential oil, await evaluation. For full evaluation, swabs should be bagged and smelled in 24 to 48 hours.

There are two more secrets to evaluating blends. First, blended fragrances age and change subtly. To approximate this change, put the bundle of swabs in a zip lock bag and test the fragrance again after a day. This will more closely approximate the ultimate fragrance that is developed. Second, since few perfumes are equal blends, complex blends are developed by using multiple swabs for the primary fragrance and fewer swabs for minor components.

How do you develop a fragrance? In perfumery, balance is generally the key. First you pick a theme. You might want a woodsy outdoor aroma or a light floral aroma or an exotic romantic aroma. Once you select your theme, read the descriptions of the fragrances. Which oils are floral, woodsy or earthy, or exotic? If you have a wide selection of oils and fragrances to choose from, write down your reaction to and evaluation of their scents. How do they fit into the category you are looking for?

For a variety of reasons, good perfumes are a balanced blend of fragrances. Each aroma has a certain characteristic, usually called a "note." The notes are indeed like music and blending is like composing. In music, you might choose a major or minor key; in fragrances that would be woodsy or floral or exotic. In piano or orchestral music, a composer does not just compose for the right hand or just for the piccolo. He seeks a balance of highs and lows, piccolo and French horn and tuba, violin and viola, and bass fiddle - a balance. Similarly, in fragrance blending there are base notes, middle notes, and top notes. And a balanced blend generally represents all three types of fragrance notes.

BASE NOTES are full, rich, earthy aromas that usually serve to anchor a blend. Many of the wood oils are base notes, like guaiac and cinnamon and vetiver. Their components are often less volatile and

they seem to cause the more volatile lighter notes to remain along with them.

TOP NOTES are light, volatile, and frequently sweet - something we might call pure and fresh, such as juniper, mint, and various citrus oils.

And finally, MIDDLE NOTES are just in between, and frequently we call these middle notes as tending to top or tending to base. Lemongrass and pine and lily of the valley are all examples of middle notes. And rose. Actually rose is a special case for many reasons. It is healing of mind and body, heart and soul. It is frequently considered a blended fragrance all by itself, with elements of base, middle, and top notes together in its fragrance. Rose is considered the perfect all around oil except for its rarity and hence its cost. Ouch.

Fragrance blending is a highly personal and subjective area. You can choose herbs and essential oils for their aromatherapy values or use what you like for a personal statement. I suggest starting with about two teaspoons of essential oil per kilogram (2.2 pounds) of oil, increasing according to taste to about three times that level. Remember that the finished soap will be less fragrant that your raw soap stock, which is probably still warm, so the addition of twice the amount of fragrance oil will not double the fragrance.

It is also important to note that single ingredient fragrances are more "effective" than blends. That is, one ounce of lavender essential oil in ten pounds of soap may produce a fully acceptable level of fragrance. However, a lavender/rosemary/lemon blend may require at least 1-1/2 total ounces

*F*AQ *How do I use the information on essential oils and herbs to make a pet shampoo or flea repellent shampoo?*

Actually a good way to start is to use any plain soap but add a few drops of lavender and/or tea tree oil to the rinse water. These oils are normally well tolerated and good for the skin. But the general approach for formulating functional soaps is to look at the list of essential oils and note how they have been used. Lavender, tea tree or manuka, rosemary, clary sage, chamomile, and lemon balm (melissa) have all been used to treat various skin problems. Therefore a soap containing several of these oils would be a good place to start. Similarly, lavender, eucalyptus, lemongrass, cypress, citranella, and pennyroyal have been used to repel insects such as fleas. In this case you would want a repellent blend that is not offensive to you if your freshly bathed pet sits down near you. That, to me, means don't add too much citronella which is quite pungent. I include specific blends in Chapter 11, Soap Recipes.

of essential oil to produce a fragrance of similar intensity. It is presumably related to the olfactory detection level of the chemical constituents of the individual oils. In music this would be equivalent to saying that an orchestra is no louder than the volume of any instrument. This is not true in sound, but does appear true in fragrance terms.

Many people approach fragrance blending as a science, selecting three oils to represent each of the three types of notes - top, middle, and base. This is fine, but remember that top notes are more volatile, fleeting, and light than middle and base notes, so it is usually advisable to physically add more of the oils representing top notes. Similarly, base notes are not only less volatile, they are frequently stronger, lingering longer than the others. Base notes, then, should represent the smallest volume added to your fragrance blend.

ESSENTIAL OILS USED FOR FRAGRANCE

The following is a list of essential oils and related products, such as extracts and medicinal herbs, that may be used (or occasionally avoided) in soapmaking. The fragrance properties are given along with reported aromatherapy uses or warnings. In most cases, blending suggestions are also given. The chemical constituents, though not obvious to most, are listed to give those familiar with chemistry a hint of the stability under saponification conditions.

ALLSPICE OR PIMENTO (pimenta officinalis). Warm, spicy, penetrating aroma, similar to cloves. Used to increase circulation, relieve tiredness and exhaustion. Blend with lavender, lemongrass, nutmeg. May cause seizing in soap. *Base to middle notes.*

ALOE VERA. Known to the Greeks in the 4th century. Used to heal burns, it is typically used as a gel; should be added at trace or rebatch. No fragrance, just nice to the skin. *No note.*

AMBER. Not exactly an essential oil as it is obtained from the destructive distillation of amber, which is a fossilized exudate of some pine trees. However, it is a staple in perfumery and has a penetrating exotic, uplifting aroma. Contains a complex mixture of terpenes. *Mostly middle notes, though I have seen it listed variously as base, middle, and middle to top, probably reflecting the variability of the material, depending on the source.*

ANGELICA (angelica archangelica). Rich herbal/earthy aroma. Once thought to be an antidote to bubonic plague, it is part of the flavor system of Chartreuse and Benedictine. Could be photo toxic (causing skin irritation if exposed to the sun). Used in treatments for headache, asthma, and stress relief; it also has a reputation for healing scars and bruises. Recommended with basil, chamomile, geranium, lavender, and citrus. Contains borneol, linalool, bergaptene, limonene, phellandrene, pinene. *Top note.*

ANISE (pimpinella anisum). Often used as a flavoring for liqueurs, candies, and baked goods due to its intense licorice flavor and taste and its carminative properties. Once used as an aphrodisiac, a reputation that modern studies may support, since it is proven sensually appealing to women. Contains up to 90% anethole plus anisaldehyde and methylchavicol. *Middle to top notes.*

BASIL (ocimum basilicum). Sweet, spicy fragrance with balsamic notes. Basil is taken from basilikon phuton, Greek for kingly herb. Antibacterial; used to clear head of colds and ease headache; used against melancholy and depression in the Middle Ages; used against stress and insomnia; considered an aphrodisiac by the Romans; reported to soothe insect bites. Recommended with bergamot, clary sage, geranium, hyssop, lavender, melissa, sandalwood, verbena. Contains linalool (40% to 50%), methyl chavicol (24%), eucalyptol, and estragol. *Middle to top notes.*

BALM (lemon) (Melissa officinalis). Lemony aroma. The modern name, melissa, is from the Greek melissophyllon, bee leaf, since melissa is the Greek word for honeybee. Lemon balm is a shortened form of lemon balsam, from the Hebrew bal-smin, meaning chief of oils. It is a component of

Aloe vera grows well indoors in pots; move it outdoors in the summer, but protect it from strong direct sunlight.

Melissa is a hardy perennial in most of the U.S. It has a tendency to spread, though, and choke other growth.

benedictine and chartreuse. Antiseptic properties promote healing of wounds, especially cuts. Used against headaches, depression, anxiety, and insomnia. Reputedly antifungal. Blends well with lavender, rose, and various citrus. Contains citronellal and geranial plus neral, citronellol, and citral. *Mostly middle notes, just a bit of top character.*

BAY (pimenta acris, laurus nobilis). Powerful spicy aroma, somewhat medicinal. A Roman symbol of wisdom and peace. Contains up to 65% to 70% phenols (chavicol, eugenol, methyl eugenol) with geraniol, linalool, terpineol, cineol, and others. Eugenol alone can account for 40% to 55% of the oil. Good respiratory aid and topical antiseptic. Used against hair loss. Victorian bay rum was obtained by distilling the leaves in rum. Sweet and spicy aroma, blends well with eucalyptus, juniper, lavender, lemon, rose, rosemary, thyme, ylang-ylang. *Base to middle notes.*

BOIS DE ROSE (aniba rosaeodora). Very sweet floral aroma with spicy character. Used to combat acne, dermatitis, wounds, general skin care (wrinkles, stretch marks, and scars). If you are concerned about tropical rain forest destruction, you might try an oil with similar chemical makeup from the Taiwan ho or shiu tree. Contains linalool (up to 97%). Blends well with lavender and rose geranium. *Middle note.*

CAJEPUT (melaleuca cajeputi). Closely related to the Australian tea tree and naioli oils. Generally used because of the antiseptic properties of the oil, but has some historical usage in herbal treat-ments of rheumatism and cholera. Although often used undiluted, some allergic reactions have been recently reported. Contains cineol (usually 50% to 60%), terpineol, pinene. *Top note.*

CAMPHOR (cinnamon camphor) white camphor. A cooling oil often used in soaps, disinfectants, etc. Obviously smells like camphor. Blends well with citrus, mint. Contains camphor, terpineol, cineol, pinene, safrol, etc. *Middle to top notes.*

CARDAMOM (elettaria cardamomum). Sweet spicy fragrance like bitter lemon with woody undertones. One of the oldest known essential oils, with reported digestive and aphrodisiac properties. Contains cineol, terpinene, terpineol, borneol, limonene, sabinene as well as linalool and linalyl acetate. Blend with geranium, juniper, lemon, rosewood, verbena. *Middle to top notes.*

CARROT SEED (daucus carota). A source of carotene (Vitamin A precursor), hence useful as an antioxidant and in treating skin disorders. Slightly sweet, dry fragrance, blends well with citrus, juniper, lavender, rosemary. Contains carotol, asarone, bisabolene, limonene, pinene. *Middle note.*

CASSIA (cinnamomum cassiac). From either leaves or bark. Woody spicy tenacious odor. Both oils contain cinnamaldehyde (75% to 90%), methyl eugenol, salicylaldehyde, methylsalicylaldehyde. Dermal toxin due to cinnamaldehyde content. *Should not be used.*

CEDAR OIL (thuja oil) (thuja plicata or occidentalis). Actually derived, not from cedar, but from arbor vitae. Sharp, camphor/evergreen aroma. Contains thujone, an oral toxin, plus fenchone and pinene. Used against plantar warts, poison ivy or oak, and as an insect repellent. It is not recommended for skin contact, but can function to repel insects. *Base note.*

CEDARWOOD OIL (juniperus virginiani). Woody, pine-like aroma. Blends with pine, rose, rosemary, vetiver. Often used to anchor or fix scent blends and is one of the oldest woods used as incense. Blends with cypress and other wood oils as well as patchouli. Used for antiseptic, skin soothing properties (sometimes applied against cellulite). Has a warm energizing fragrance. Contains cedrene and cedral. *Mostly base to middle notes.*

CHAMOMILE Roman (anthemis nobilis, now chamaemelum nobile). Warm, fruity aroma. Has been in continuous use from the time of the Egyptians, who dedicated it to the gods. Its name is derived from the Greek chamaimelon or apple on the ground due to its strong apple scent. It is variously recommended for external use against sores, acne, allergies, boils, cuts, eczema, inflammations, rashes, toothaches, migraines, neuralgia, to ease anxiety, and treat insomnia. It is still used today in hair preparations to lighten and condition hair. Blends well with angelica, geranium, lavender, lemon, palmarosa, patchouli, rose, ylang-ylang. Contains esters of angelic and tiglic acids (about 85%) with pinene, azulene, farnesol, and other constituents. *Middle to top notes.*

CHAMOMILE German (matricaria chamomilla). Also called blue chamomile from the characteristic blue color of the azulene, which is formed during steam distillation. Characteristic aroma. See Chamomile, Roman. *Middle to top notes.*

CINNAMON (cinnamomum zeylanicum or verum). Available from leaves or inner bark. Warm spicy aroma. Blends well with mandarin (actually most citrus oils) and clove. Leaf contains eugenol (80% to 96%), cinnamaldehyde (3%), linalool, safrol; bark contains cinnamaldehyde (40% to 50%) eugenol (4% to 10%), benzaldehyde, pinene, cineol, cymene, others. The bark oil is a dermal toxin and should not be used; the leaf oil should be used with caution as it may cause chemical sensitization. *Base to middle notes.*

CITRONELLA (cymbopogon nardus). Powerful woody sweet lemony fragrance. Insect repellent and used in Chinese herbal medicine for rheumatic pain relief. Antiseptic, fungicidal action. Composition varies widely depending on place of origin. Contains geraniol (up to 45%), citronellol (up to 50%) plus geranyl acetate, limonene, camphene. Blend with geranium, citrus, cedar - can be overwhelming. *Top note.*

CLARY SAGE (salvia sclaria). Sweet, nutty herbaceous aroma. Blends well with citrus, fir, lavender. Primarily grown as a flavoring for muscatel. In the 16th century, it was considered to be an aphrodisiac. Its name is from the Latin clarus for its use to relieve tired, sore eyes. It is also used to combat general fatigue and depression and

Arbor vitae, the source of cedar oil, has a wide range of growth zones and is often grown as a wind break or border.

German chamomile is an annual (which sometimes will reseed itself,) but Roman chamomile (shown) is a somewhat tender perennial. The flowers are easy to harvest and dry and are wonderful additions ground and added to soap.

Both the root and dried leaf of comfrey have medicinal uses. Once established in your garden, it can be hard to contain this vigorous herb.

to condition and darken thinning hair. An ancient Latin saying was "cur morietur homo, cui salvia crescit in horto? (How can a man die who has sage growing in his garden?)" Contains linalyl acetate (up to 75%), linalool, pinene, and others. Used for acne, wrinkles, muscle aches. *Middle to top notes.*

CLOVE (eugenia caryophyllata). The name is from the Latin clavus, meaning nail shaped. Strong spicy penetrating odor. Medicinal history dates to Greeks, Romans, and Chinese. Used to relieve pain, strengthen memory, lift depression. Possible antiseptic for treating skin sores and wounds. Blend with basil, cinnamon, lemon, nutmeg, orange, rosemary. Contains furfural, methyl salicylate, eugenol (82% to 87% including about 10% acetyleugenol), caryophyllene, pinene. May cause soap to seize due to its eugenol content. *Middle note.*

COFFEE (coffee arabica and species). Used as the essential oil, as strongly brewed coffee, or even as finely ground spent grounds. Uplifting characteristic fragrance; often used (in soap) to combat odors on hands and feet; although the coffee aroma fades in soap, it is reportedly still useful in combating odors. *Middle note.*

COMFREY (symphytum officinale). Also known as boneset or knitbone. The name is probably from the Roman conferva to join together. It is used against swelling, sprains, bruises, neuralgia and to promote healing of broken bones and sores. Some reports indicate that the mucilage content of its root, used as a poultice, dried to form a mass which would hold broken bones in place.

Contains asparagin. Leaves as well as powdered root are used; not an essential oil. *No fragrance notes.*

CYPRESS (cupressus sempervirens). Refreshing woodsy fragrance. Uses claimed include deodorant, antiseptic, and insect repellent as well as astringent properties against cellulite and varicose veins. Blends well with various citrus and fir oils. Contains pinene, camphene, terpineol, furfural, cymene, cedrol. *Definite middle note.*

EUCALYPTUS (eucalyptus globulous). Sharp and penetrating, spicy camphorous odor. Bactericide, antiviral, insect repellent, parasiticide, burns, pulmonary conditions. Contains eucalyptol or cineole (80% to 85%), phellandrene, pinene, camphene, others. Blends with coriander, juniper, lavender, lemongrass, melissa, thyme. There are now several variants available as essential oils with similar pulmonary effects, but much milder and hence safer, such as lemon eucalyptus (eucalyptus citriodora). *Top note.*

FEVERFEW (chrysanthemum parthenium). Its name reflects the Latin febrifugia, a substance which drives out fevers. Traditionally used to treat fevers, relieve insect bites, calm nerves. It is also used as a moth repellent. Contains camphor. Ordinarily used as ground herb or a tea, not an essential oil. *No fragrance notes.*

FRANKINCENSE (boswellia thurifera). Also called Olibanum for Lebanon Oil. It has a warm spicy woody aroma. It is used as a perfume fixative and, of course, incense. Traditional use to produce a calm, meditative state, ease shortness of breath, etc. Blends well with citrus and exotics and wood fragrances such as patchouli, sandalwood, and pine. Contains cadinene, camphene, pinene, phellandrene, and olibanol. *Middle to base notes.*

GERANIUM (pelargonium graveolens or odorantissimum) "Rose Geranium." Sweet heavy odor reminiscent of roses. Blends well with lavender, rose, and patchouli. Pelargonium is derived from the Greek for stork's bill reflecting the fruit's shape. To produce a single pound of essential oil, 300 to 500 pounds of plant material are required. It is reportedly an antiseptic and analgesic. Relieves stress, depression, acne, athlete's foot, hemorrhoids, bruises, cuts, burns, dermatitis, etc. Contains citronellol, geraniol esters (20% to 35%), linalool, isomenthone, menthone. Blend with angelica, basil, bay, sage, lavender, petitgrain, rose, rosemary, sandalwood. *Base to middle notes.*

GUAIACWOOD (bulnesia sarmienti). Deep, earthy, smoky fragrance. Reported to help tighten and rejuvenate aging skin. Often used with rose-like fragrances and citrus. Contains bulnesol and guaiol. *Base notes.*

HELICHRYSUM (helichrysum angustifolium). One of the major essential oils, though there are hundreds of individual species grown. Mostly used for tremendous skin healing properties, this essential oil is generally much too costly for use in soap. Also called Immortelle, Everlasting, and Strawflower. Contains geraniol, linalool, nerol, and pinene. *Middle to top notes.*

HOPS (humulus lupulus). Rich, spicy sweet aroma. Calming and sleep inducing. Flowers, along with chamomile, are used as a soothing poultice for rheumatic joints. Also against dermatitis, rough skin, asthma, with some reported use in aphrodisiacs (possibly when present with fermented grain extracts). Anti-microbial, antiseptic, pleasantly narcotic. For rheumatic joints, neuralgia, antibiotic contains (65% to 70%) humulene, myrcene, caryophyllene and farnesene. *Middle notes.*

HYSSOP (hyssopus officinalis). Sweet, penetrating warm herbal

A number of scented geranium varieties are available for the home gardener. They are not hardy but make good houseplants during the winter.

There are hundreds of helichrysum species and most are easy-to-grow annuals. Shown is the species called strawflower that produces the wonderful healing oil.

This hops vine growing along my fence has withstood accidental mowing and still thrives. Just find it a good fence or trellis. The dried flowers are ground and used in beer and soap.

Blue, white, and pink varieties of hyssop are available for the garden. Easy-to-grow perennials.

aroma. Flowers attractive to bees. From Hebrew Ezop meaning good scented herb. Eases sprains and rheumatic joints and promotes quick healing of cuts and sores, bruises, dermatitis. Reputed to have a strong therapeutic effect on the mind. Contains about 50% pinene, pinocamphone, isopino-camphone, borneol, camphor, thujone, cadinene, others. Blend with angelica, lavender, melissa, rosemary, tangerine. *Middle notes.*

JASMINE (jasminum officinale and related species and varieties). Available as the absolute or fragrance oil, not true essential oil, although prior to the late 1980s very small quantities of an essential oil were produced. Warm uplifting sensuous floral fragrance, called the "king of perfumes or flower oils" with soothing and calming properties. Blend with mandarin, lavender, rose. Contains farnesol, geraniol, nerol, terpineol, jasmone, eugenol. *Mostly base notes.*

JUNIPER (juniperus communis). Characterized by the sweet, balsamic odor characteristic of gin. Widespread medicinal use in Tibet, Rome, Greece, and Arabia. Used against eczema, acne, sores, ulcers, dermatosis, and rheumatism or aching joints. It is an antiseptic and parasiticide. Contains borneol, isoborneol, cadinene, pinene, camphene, terpineol, and others. Blends with citrus, geranium, rosemary, sandalwood, various firs. *Top and middle notes.*

LAVANDIN (lavandula fragrans or intermedia). Aroma similar to lavender, but more penetrating. This hybrid species is a cross between true lavender and aspic, or spike lavender. Whereas lavender is calming and relaxing, lavandin is more stimulating and energizing. A single pound of essential oils is produced from approximately 35 pounds of flowers. Contains linalool, linalyl acetate, camphor, cineole, camphene, limonene, etc. Blend with bergamot, chamomile, clary sage, geranium. *Middle to top notes.*

LAVENDER (lavandula angustifolia) English Lavender. Floral aroma with woody undertones. From the Latin lavare, to wash. Romans added it to their baths for antiseptic and insect repellent properties. Traditional uses include calming nerves, easing sprains and rheumatic pains, and promoting hair growth. Probably due to antiseptic properties, it is used against abscesses, acne, dermatitis, eczema, insect bites, ringworm, sores, wounds, rheumatism, sprains, and especially burns. A 1995 article in the *Lancet* (a British medical journal) extols the ability of lavender to regulate sleep patterns in people who are being temporarily taken off sleep regulating medication. One of the most important essential oils; one pound of oil is produced from about 100 pounds of flowers. Contains up to 40% linalyl acetate, linalool, terpineol, limonene, geraniol, cineol, borneol, caryophyllene. Blends with bay, bergamot, chamomile, clary sage, eucalyptus, geranium, nutmeg, patchouli, thyme, rosemary. *Definitely middle notes but with base and top notes that can vary depending on year and source.*

LEMON (citrus limonum). Refreshing, uplifting, penetrating fragrance. Used for astringent properties and oily skin. Contains limonene, terpinene, citral, linalool, geraniol, and related compounds. Blends well with other citrus fragrances as well as spicy fragrances (clove, cinnamon, cardamom, etc.). Avoid exposure to sunlight after direct contact due to possible photosensitivity. Contains limonene, terpinene, phellandrene, pinene, citral. *Top notes.*

LEMONGRASS (cymbopogon citratus). Strong lemony aroma, somewhat grassy/earthy. With rosemary for aches and pains; strongly antiseptic, antibacterial, antifungal; flea and tick repellent. Contains 75% to 85% citral, citranellal, limonene, dipentene, methylheptanone, farnesol, nerol. Stimulating and revitalizing. Blend with basil, coriander, geranium, lavender, neroli, Palmarosa, rosemary, tea tree, litsea cubeba. *Middle and top notes.*

LILY OF VALLEY (convallaria majalis). Beautiful, clear floral aroma. Traditionally used to clear the mind or restore memory. *Middle note.*

LINDEN (tilia europaea). Sweet, long-lasting aroma. The Linden tree (usually called basswood in the U. S.) is the symbol of the Germanic nation. Contains farnesol. Sleep promoting, often in combination with hops. Used against burns and blemishes. Blend with lavender, neroli, palmarosa, rose, verbena, violet, ylang-ylang. Mostly available as an extract. *Middle note.*

LITSEA CUBEBA (litsea cubeba). Essential oil with a very high citral content often added to extend the citrus aroma of other essential oils which tend not to survive the high alkalinity of saponification. Contains geraniol, linalool, citral, cineole, cadinene, limonene, sabinene. *Lemony top notes.*

MANUKA (leptospermum coparium). Also known as New Zealand tea tree. This oil is fairly new to commercialization, though it has been used for centuries by the Maoris for its healing properties. *Top note.*

MARIGOLD (calendula officinalis). African or pot marigold. Sharp, herbaceous aroma. Assists the healing of wounds including burns and leg ulcers; smoothing to face and hands (chapped). Contains calendulin (resin) waxes and oil. Not to be confused with the common marigold (tagetes). *Top note.*

MARJORAM (origanum marjorana). Warm, woody, spicy, and camphorous aroma. Increases circulation, treats bruises; soporific; soothes pain, especially muscles and joints. The Greek goddess Aphrodite supposedly used marjoram to cure the wounds of her son, Aeneus. Contains terpinene, terpineol, borneol, camphor, pinene, caryophylline. Blend with bergamot, chamomile, lavender, nutmeg, rosemary, ylang-ylang. *Middle note.*

NEROLI OIL (citrus aurantium). Warm, sweet floral fragrance. Used for skin rejuvenation, sleep aid, relieving chronic anxiety and depression. The prohibitive expense of this essential oil is a result of the yield: it takes about 1,000 pounds of flowers (from the bitter orange tree) to produce one pound of oil. Contains nerol, geraniol, linalool, terpineol, linalyl acetate (7% to 18%), methyl anthranilate, jasmone, camphene,

There are several varieties of lavender (shown) available to the home gardener. Check the growth zone carefully for hardiness.

The Linden tree or American basswood is noted for its wood, used for carving, and its delicately sweet fragrant flowers that appear in late June and early July.

Calendula or pot marigold is an easy to grow border annual. The dried flower heads, source of the essential oil, will give soap a yellow to gold color.

Huge fields of peppermint are grown in the U.S. for essential oil production, but many other varieties, such as the chocolate mint shown, are available for the home garden. Photo by Deb Shuman.

Many mint varieties are available for home gardeners. Shown is chocolate mint, a wonderful fragrance.

limonene. Blend with bergamot, coriander, geranium, lavender, palmarosa, petitgrain, rosemary, sandalwood, ylang-ylang. *Middle to top notes.*

NIAOULI OIL (see Tea Tree oil). Clear penetrating camphorous aroma. Strongly antiseptic, it is used for skin irritations and in veterinary medicine as a rub for rheumatic dog limbs. Contains valeric acid, cineole (up to about 65%), terpineol, limonene, pinene. Blend with coriander, juniper, lavender, peppermint, rosemary. *Top note.*

NUTMEG (myristica fragrans). Sharp spicy aroma. The oil comes from the seed kernel; mace is the husk. Stimulant, hair tonic. This oil is a warming oil and care must be taken to use only small amounts or avoid sensitive skin areas. Contains borneol, geraniol (6%), linalool, terpineol, eugenol, safrole, camphene (60% to 80%), pinene, myristicin (4%), elemicin (25%). Blend with cinnamon, clove, coriander, melissa, patchouli, rosemary, tea tree. *Middle note.*

PALMAROSA (cymbopogon martini). Sweet, floral aroma with slight rose character. Contains geraniol (75% to 95%), citronellol, farnesol, and others. Used against skin conditions like acne, wrinkles (from sun exposure), and for broken veins. Reputed to refresh and clarify the mind. Contains geraniol, citronellol, farnesol, citral, citronellal, geranyl acetate, limonene. Blend with bergamot, geranium, lavender, melissa, petitgrain, rosewood, sandalwood, ylang-ylang. *Middle note.*

PARSLEY (petroselinum sativum). Grassy, herbal aroma. Used against cystitis, rheumatism, sore eyes, wounds, broken capillaries. Contains terpinene, pinene, apiol, and others. Blend with lavender, marjoram, rosemary, thyme, sage, and most citrus oils. *Top note.*

PATCHOULI (pogostemon cablin). Strong, penetrating sweet, musky and spicy fragrance. Long history of medical use in Malaysia, China, India, and Japan and equally long use as an aphrodisiac. It is used as an antiseptic as well as an insecticide. Uses include actions against acne, athlete's foot, dandruff, dermatitis, eczema, sores, wounds. Contains patchouli alcohol (about 40%) plus pogostol, bulnesol, and others. Blend with bergamot, clary sage, geranium, lavender, lemongrass, neroli, rosewood, peppermint. *Base to middle notes.*

PEPPERMINT (mentha piperita). A stimulating and uplifting characteristic refreshing fragrance. According to Roman mythology, the nymph Menthe (or minthe), casualty of an ancient love triangle, was changed into the herb by Pluto. Contains menthol in excess of 50%, carvone, menthone, limonene, pulegone, cineol. Blend with juniper, spearmint, patchouli, rosemary, lavender, tea tree. Excessive amounts can be skin irritants. *Middle to top notes.*

PETITGRAIN OIL (citrus aurantium). Fresh floral citrus aroma. Often used in combination with Neroli. One of three essential oils from the orange tree, this oil derived from the leaves. It is reported to clear confusion, depression, mental fatigue. Possible photosensitivity may result if used prior to exposure to sun. Contains (40% to 80%)

linalyl acetate, geraniol, geranyl acetate, limonene. Blend with bergamot, cardamom, geranium, lavender, melissa, palmarosa, rosemary, rosewood, neroli, ylang-ylang. *Top note.*

PINE (pinus sylvestris). Fresh woodsy fir aroma. Often used for deodorant effect and to increase blood circulation, but can cause skin irritation in high concentration. Contains pinene, cadinene, bornyl acetate, sylvestrene, dipentene. Blends well with cedarwood, sandalwood, guiacwood, cypress. *Middle note.*

ROSE (rose otto from rosa damascena and related species). Tremendously uplifting, rich floral fragrance, with hundreds of minor chemical components in this oil along with up to 70% geraniol. This is one of the oldest (and most expensive) of the essential oils; roughly 4,400 pounds of rose blossoms are needed to produce a single pound of essential oil. Myths relating to roses abound, but it is a noted symbol of silence - a rose suspended over a table was a sign that the discussions held were to be kept secret by all participants, hence the term "sub rosa" (under the rose). Widely used in perfumery and cosmetics both to improve the fragrance bouquet and for the soothing properties to mind and skin. Blend with other floral oils. *Middle plus top and base notes.*

ROSEMARY (rosmarinus officinalis) "dew of the sea" from Corsica and Sardinia. Strong penetrating, woody, camphorous, or balsamic aroma. Used with thyme to treat dandruff. It has been found in the Egyptian tombs, probably as a result of its antioxidant, preservative qualities or possibly due to its use to stimulate and rejuvenate skin. Contains pinenes, camphene, limonene, cineol, borneol (10+%), and so on. Used to treat acne, dandruff, eczema, asthma, rheumatism, poor circulation, and to soothe nerves and promote hair growth. Used by Egyptians, Greeks, Romans. Blend with basil, geranium, lavender, lemongrass, melissa, peppermint, tangerine. *Middle to top notes.*

SAGE (salvia officinalis). Warm spicy herbaceous and slightly camphorous aroma. Quickens senses and memory, strengthens sinews. Used for palsy and trembling, rheumatic joints and sciatica, and with chamomile to relieve asthma attacks. Mainly thujone (42%) cineol, borneol, and other terpenes, it should be used only with caution and is usually replaced by Clary sage. *Top note.*

SANDALWOOD (santalum album). This oil had to be included since it is such a favorite and has been used in religious rites for centuries, both as incense and even in the construction of temples. Musky rich exotic oil, high quality fresh oils have little fragrance but reportedly fragrance builds with time and possibly with exposure to air. Used for skin and hair care. Blends well with rose, jasmine, lavender, patchouli, and other exotics. Contains forneol, santalone, and related compounds. *Full of base notes.*

SELF HEAL (prunella vulgaris). Frequently use to stem blood from accidents and fights due to its styptic properties. Not known as an essential oil; use as ground herb or tea. *No fragrance notes.*

This is the prime rose for the distillation of rose otto essential oil. However, many very fragrant varieties are available in the U.S. which can be used for infusion. Photo by Butch Owen.

The rosemary shown in bloom here was pot grown and successfully wintered with slight protection in zone 6.

Thyme is a wonderful culinary and medicinal herb that can be grown in pots in the kitchen window or as a garden perennial.

SPEARMINT (mentha viridas). Warm herbaceous minty aroma. Mild antiseptic, acne, skin irritations, headache, nausea, antidepressant, mental strain, fatigue. Contains (50%+) carvone, limonene, pinene. Blends well with peppermint and various citrus oils. *Middle to top notes.*

SPIKE LAVENDER (lavandula latifolia or spica, also called aspic). Like lavandin, this oil is energizing rather than calming. Traditional uses against rheumatism, arthritis. Contains cineole (ca. 35%) and camphor (40% to 60%) with linalool, borneol, terpineol, and camphene. Aroma similar to lavender, but more camphorous. Eases breathing and clears a stuffy head. Blend as with lavender. *Middle and top notes.*

TEA TREE (melaleuca alternifolia). Closely related to cajeput (melaleuca cajeputi) and niaouli (melaleuca viridiflora). Spicy camphorous, somewhat balsamic odor. Can be blended with lavender, peppermint, and fir oils, more to disguise its own odor than enhance the other. Used against abscesses, acne, athlete's foot, herpes, rashes, plantar warts, insect bites, sinusitis, asthma, bronchitis, burns and sunburns, lice, antifungal treatment against tinea, pedis, ringworm, candida. One pound of oil is distilled from about 45 pounds of leaves. Contains terpinene-4-ol (up to 30%), viridiflorene, cineol, pinene, terpinenes, cymene, and others. Reportedly absorbed through skin; has anesthetic properties. 1933 *British Medical Journal* reported it was a powerful disinfectant; 1955 reported in U.S. that it was actively germicidal. *Top notes.*

THYME (thymus vulgaris). Powerful warm spicy herbaceous odor. Blends with citrus, lavender, pine, rosemary. Has strong antiseptic properties due to thymol in oil. It has varied uses including the treatment of stuffy nose, fatigue, skin sores and pimples, burns, insect bites, rheumatism, and with rosemary for dandruff. Contains thymol and carvacrol (up to 60%) with cymene, terpinene, camphene, borneol, linalool, and some others. It was used by the Sumarians, Egyptians, and Romans who thought it dispelled melancholy and promoted bravery; it was often carried to prevent airborne diseases. From the Greek Thumos for smell or perfume. *Middle note.*

VERBENA OIL (lippia citriodora or aloysia triphylla). Sweet lemony floral fruity aroma. A South American plant introduced to Europe by the Spanish. It has been used to treat acne and to aid in relaxation. It is especially used with rosemary and lavender. Contains citral (30% to 35%), geraniol, nerol, others. Possible phototoxicity due to citral content. *Top note.*

VETIVER OIL (andropogon zizanioides). Sweet woody earthy fragrance. Moisturizing, stimulates circulation for arthritis. Used for dry irritated mature or aging skin. Calming and sedating. Contains vetiverols (45% to 65%), vetivene, 8% to 35% ketones including vetivones. Often used as a base or fixative for fragrance blends. It takes almost 300 pounds of this grass to produce a single pound of oil. *Full base note.*

VIOLET FLOWER/LEAF OIL (viola odorata). Sweet rich floral

fragrance. It has been cultivated for over 2,000 years as a coloring agent and source of perfume. Various reported uses include treatment of skin inflammation, rheumatism, to encourage sleep and relieve headache. Contains saponins, violarutin, methyl salicylate, others. *Middle note.*

WINTERGREEN (gualtheria promcumbens). Strong characteristic minty aroma. Contains mainly methyl salicylate. Can be absorbed through skin and may contribute to salicylate poisoning when overused or used in conjunction with other salicylates, including aspirin. Often used as a counter-irritant in pharmaceutical rubs to draw blood to bruised skin and especially sore joints. Use only with caution. *Top note.*

YLANG-YLANG (cananga odorata) "flower of flowers," "queen of perfumes" (and poor man's jasmine as well). Intensely sweet floral, somewhat spicy aroma. Pronounced ee-long, ee-long. I found these flower buds used in both Taiwan and Thailand in strings to be hung in automobiles as natural air fresheners. In Thailand they were strung together in long strands with rose petals and jasmine buds. Wow! Used as part of dry scalp treatment and for dry aging skin. Antidepressant, antiseptic, aphrodisiac, insomnia, relief of nervous depression, anxiety. Ylang-ylang is often available in several varieties, referring to how it is distilled as well as the quality of the oil. Do not be surprised to see something called ylang-ylang II (or 2) or III (3); each version is a bit different, so evaluate the cost and the scent of each. I personally think a good soap would be one scented with ylang-ylang

and containing witch hazel, which would obviously be called ylang-ylang, the witch is dead soap. Contains geraniol and linalool acetates and benzoates, cadinenes, p-cresol methyl ether. Blends well with lavender, rosemary, and other florals. *Middle note.*

Violets are easy to grow, except of course for the fragrant varieties which are quite tender and not as showy as this species from the shaded part of our gardens.

FAQ

WHAT ARE THE MOST POPULAR FRAGRANCES?

Obviously the answer depends on your audience, but the most popular essential oils selected by over 100 people working in or familiar with the field of aromatherapy are:

1. *Lavender*
2. *Sandalwood*
3. *Peppermint*
4. *Eucalyptus*
5. *Rosemary*
6. *Tea Tree*
7. *Geranium*
8. *Rose*
9. *Citrus (Bergamot, Lemon, Neroli, Grapefruit, Orange, Tangerine, Lime)*
10. *Clary Sage*
11. *Frankincense*
12. *Patchouli*
13. *Chamomile*

These selections reflect a combination of beneficial properties which include, but are by no means limited to, aroma. I can say, though, that these do reflect the most requested fragrances available as herbs and essential oils.

Not all beautiful natural scents are available as essential oils. Although a lilac scent can be prepared by infusion or enfleurage, for a pronounced scent in your soap you will have to use a fragrance oil.

Hyacinth gives one of the most intense sweet fragrances of early spring. Definitely a candidate as a base to prepare an infused oil.

Fragrance oils, especially for those scents not available (economically) from essential oils, represent another series of favorites.

1. Vanilla
2. Rose
3. Jasmine
4. Lilac
5. Gardenia
6. Almond
7. Apple
8. Chocolate
9. Musk
10. Cucumber
11. Raspberry

The only factor that usually inhibits creativity in blending fragrances is the cost of the essential or fragrance oils. However, with the ability to use cotton swabs to preview your fragrance blends, you can be creative without being wasteful. It is also helpful that many suppliers will offer a limited number of free or quite low cost small samples for you to evaluate. Of course, the more expensive the oil, the smaller the sample, but it does provide an opportunity to confirm your hope that you can blend your own winning fragrance.

FAQ

WHAT ARE YOUR FAVORITE BLENDS?

These are my favorite fragrance blends that require only two or three scents. The numbers refer to drops of each scent in the blend. And remember - rose blends with almost anything and almost everything blends with rose.

1. *Luscious lavender - 3 lavender/1 rosemary*
2. *JuicyMint - 3 grapefruit/1 spearmint*
3. *Timeless - 3 patchouli/1 peppermint*
4. *Plenty-Good - 3 cucumber/1 anise*
5. *Holiday Punch - 2 cinnamon/1 orange*
6. *DublMint - 2 peppermint/1 spearmint*
7. *English Garden - 2 to 3 lavender/1 rosewood*
8. *Mint Patty - 2 to 3 chocolate/1 peppermint*
9. *Wink - 3 juniper berry/1 grapefruit or bergamot*
10. *Peppy Mint - 4 tea tree/1 peppermint*
11. *Royal Bouquet - 4 ylang-ylang II/2 lavender/1 palmarosa/1 rosemary*
12. *Pine Barrens - 3 white pine/1 cypress/1 cedarwood/1/2 guaiac*
13. *Lavender Rose - 4 lavender/1 palmarosa/1 rosewood*
14. *Herb Garden - 4 rosemary/1 thyme/1 clary sage*
15. *Heaven Scent - 4 ylang-ylang II /1 jasmine/1/2 to 1 rose*
16. *Chocolate Chip Cookie - 2 brown sugar/1 vanilla/1/2 chocolate*
17. *Blueberry Muffin - 2 brown sugar/1 vanilla/1/2 blueberry*

CHAPTER 11
SOAP RECIPES

Since soap can be made from almost any fat or oil, why develop a recipe? Why not use whatever is at hand, just like the pioneers did? Once you try a few basic recipes and gain confidence in making soap, you will probably want to spread your wings and try other oils, additives, and combinations. These recipes use the temperatures and conditions given in Chapter 7. Most of the combinations given here are three or more oils in order to give a balance of properties (hardness, lather, mildness) in the finished soap.

In general, the colors and fragrances used in a soap are not a requirement of the basic recipe. Fragrances are discussed in detail in Chapter 10, though I have made a few suggestions for the optional addition of some essential oils. Remember that herbs, fragrances, colorants, and preservatives are all added "at trace," the point where the batch thickens to the point where the soap stays in suspension and any residual oil and water (lye solution) no longer separate into layers.

My own soap recipes are based on blends of olive, coconut, soy or canola, and palm oils. As I developed these recipes, I wrote a computer spreadsheet to help me calculate the fatty acid distribution available from a blend of oils. I knew that I needed to have at least 15% by weight of coconut oil for good sudsing, but over 50% could result in a harsh soap. Trial and error with oil content and reaction conditions (of course, I meant to say a carefully designed experimental plan followed by in-depth statistical analysis of the results) gave me a soap that exceeded my original demands and expectations.

My recipes are geared to make good soap in reasonable time. I have tried to balance the fatty acid distribution by means of these blends to have enough lauric acid (from coconut) to provide good lathering, enough long chain fatty acids from olive and soy for good oily soil removal and mildness, and enough palm oil to provide hardness and density in the finished bar.

Most of my recipes do not use tallow or lard (beef and pork fat respectively) for several reasons:
1. Animal fats are objectionable to some people for a variety of health, ethical, or religious reasons. Since I sell my soap, I do not want to alienate any potential consumers.
2. The odor of animal fats is not as bland as the odor of vegetable oils, which makes scenting more difficult.
3. Although lard is available in most grocery stores, tallow must either be rendered from butcher's scraps or purchased from a meat packer or broker, i.e. it is hard to get in a directly usable form. On the other hand, if you have access to a local supply of fats, you can substitute lard or tallow for some or all of the palm and soy oils in my recipes, making the appropriate adjustments in the amount of lye required. Tallow or a mixture of tallow and lard is used in most commercial soaps and can make an outstanding cold process soap and one that is easily rebatched. Furthermore, a soap made with a high lard content is very useful in the laundry, especially to pretreat stubborn soils and stains. If you don't mind the extra work, lard, which is readily available, is an extremely useful tool in your soap design arsenal.

FAQ

MY BUTCHER CAN GIVE ME TALLOW FOR ALMOST NOTHING. WHAT DO I NEED TO DO TO IT BEFORE I CAN USE IT IN SOAP?

Tallow, hard beef fat, needs to be purified or rendered before use in soap. The easiest way I know is to put the tallow in a large stock pot and add roughly a cup of water and three tablespoons of salt for every pound of tallow. Bring this to a boil and keep it boiling for a half hour, then cool it to room temperature and place it in the refrigerator until the top tallow layer has solidified. Remove this solid tallow and scrape off any dark material on the bottom (this will be meat residue and other proteinaceous material). I recommend taking this top layer and repeating the boiling and cooling treatment, this time using a cup of water and two to three tablespoons of baking soda per pound. You can now take this solid layer and use it for soap; keep it refrigerated or frozen if you do not use it right away, since it will spoil.

For those who do not want to use either tallow or lard and who do not have access to palm oil, consider vegetable shortening, especially if made from cottonseed oil. Due to nutrition concerns, cottonseed oil accounts for only about 3% of oils used to make shortening in the U.S. today. However, the fatty acid distribution of partially hydrogenated cottonseed oil is quite similar to lard and shortenings containing all or mostly partially hydrogenated cottonseed oil are good substitutes. In general, switching between most vegetable shortenings (made mostly from partially hydrogenated soybean oil) and lard will work, but the substitution is not as close a fit.

Although I do make some superfatted soap, the bulk of the soap I produce has nearly a 1:1 ratio of fatty acids to lye. People with dry skin can tolerate, even need, extra emollients, while others may break out as a result of the extra oil. Highly superfatted soaps will often need the addition of antioxidants since they can become rancid (dry soap will resist rancidity since bacterial growth requires moisture) when left in contact with water. The simplest antioxidants are natural oils which are sources of Vitamin A or E. Wheat germ oil and carrot seed oil are suitable natural sources. Grapefruit seed extract is sometimes used, with the extra benefit of shortening the overall reaction time for saponification, though one should not rely totally on grapefruit seed extract to avoid rancidity and off colors. Rosemary oil extract (ROE) is also becoming readily available and has a well documented history of commercial use in stabilizing oils and oil derivatives. It is probably the most promising antioxidant now entering the market.

You may also find Vitamin E or Vitamin E oil at your drugstore. Vitamin E oil is simply Vitamin E which is supplied in a vegetable oil carrier; and the carrier oil should be included in your lye calculations. Vitamin C, ascorbic acid, is also an antioxidant. However, ascorbic acid will consume lye, approximately 0.23 grams of lye will be neutralized for every gram of ascorbic acid added. Depending on your recipe, you might need to add enough additional lye to neutralize the added ascorbic acid. Most vitamins are available in natural or synthetic forms. The effectiveness of synthetic forms can vary according to the nature of the synthetic and the desired function.

BASIC FOUR OIL SOAP I

Nothing fancy here, just a good blend of oils that make good soap. Add your herbs or fragrance oils at trace (refer to page 49). I have indicated the ingredient weights in ounces in parentheses. *Remember, these are **weights**, not volumes.*

OK, basic soap is white and boring. Here is a basic soap poured into a loofa (which was wrapped tightly with plastic wrap so the soap would not run out before it solidified). The soap-filled loofa was sliced into sections using a serrated knife.

Coconut Oil	725 grams (25.57 oz.)
Palm Oil	775 grams (27.39 oz.)
Canola Oil	650 grams (22.93 oz.)
Olive Oil	150 grams (5.29 oz.)
Lye	12 oz. dissolved in 700 grams (24.7 oz.) distilled or deionized water

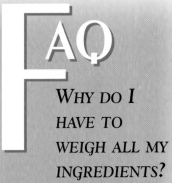

FAQ

Why do I have to weigh all my ingredients?

Chemical reactions, such as saponification, are based on the molecular weights of all the chemicals that react. Measuring cups and similar volume measuring devices are not accurate enough to assure that the correct amounts of the ingredients are used. Since lye is very harsh, it is important to be sure the correct amount is used in a recipe and this means weighing the ingredients.

Basic Four Oil Soap II

This soap is tinted with turmeric to give it an interesting peachy color, which goes well with peach or apricot fragrance oil. Start with three tablespoons of fragrance oil in this size batch.

This is similar to the previous recipe, except for the substitution of soybean oil for canola. Both are low cost oils that produce a mild soap, though people with soy allergies may want to stick with the canola formula. I have indicated the ingredient weights in ounces in parentheses. *Remember, these are **weights**, not volumes.*

COCONUT OIL	1500 GRAMS (52.91 OZ.)
OLIVE OIL	400 GRAMS (14.11 OZ.)
SOYBEAN OIL	1460 GRAMS (51.50 OZ.)
PALM OIL	1000 GRAMS (35.27 OZ.)
LYE	24 OZ. DISSOLVED IN 1400 GRAMS (49.38 OZ.) DISTILLED OR DEIONIZED WATER

Basic Three Oil Soap

Turmeric gives the basic color while powdered kelp produces the nice green.

This is a premium soap made with a high olive oil content for mildness plus coconut oil for lather and all-vegetable shortening instead of the harder-to-find palm oil for hardness. These are probably the three easiest ingredients to find when starting out and they make an excellent soap. This recipe will produce a very white soap unless you select a dark green olive oil, which will give it a greenish cast. The weights in ounces are indicated in parentheses. *Remember, these are **weights**, not volumes.*

COCONUT OIL	750 GRAMS (26.46 OZ.)
OLIVE OIL	750 GRAMS (26.46 OZ.)
SHORTENING	900 GRAMS (31.75 OZ.)
LYE	12 OZ. DISSOLVED IN 650 GRAMS (22.93 OZ.) DISTILLED OR DEIONIZED WATER

BASIC THREE OIL SOAP II

When I made this batch I tried out some shocking pink soap color tabs; I added shavings of the tab and mixed them in until I got the color I wanted. The melt and pour color base melts nicely in this cold process soap at trace. Try a strawberry fragrance oil to go with the color.

I know that some would prefer to begin making soap using a lower cost oil instead of olive oil. This recipe substitutes canola oil for the olive, but in this case, the amount of shortening must be increased to maintain the hardness and texture of the soap. The weights in ounces are indicated in parentheses. *Remember, these are **weights**, not volumes.*

COCONUT OIL	750 GRAMS (26.46 OZ.)
CANOLA OIL	700 GRAMS (24.69 OZ.)
SHORTENING	1000 GRAMS (35.27 OZ.)
LYE	12 OZ. DISSOLVED IN 650 GRAMS (22.93 OZ.) DISTILLED OR DEIONIZED WATER

Basic Soap With Beeswax

This nice piece of molded beeswax was a gift from beekeeper friends.

Beeswax is often added to hand soaps since it provides extra softening action for rough red hands. It also provides the soapmaker with an added benefit by promoting thickening during saponification, so this is a good additive for beginners afraid their soap won't solidify. The weights in ounces are indicated in parentheses. *Remember, these are **weights**, not volumes.*

BEESWAX	50 GRAMS (1.76 OZ.)
OLIVE OIL	350 GRAMS (12.35 OZ.)
COCONUT OIL	1300 GRAMS (45.86 OZ.)
SOYBEAN OIL	1400 GRAMS (49.38 OZ.)
PALM OIL	300 GRAMS (10.58 OZ.)
LYE	24 OZ. DISSOLVED IN 1400 GRAMS (49.38 OZ.) DISTILLED OR DEIONIZED WATER

BASIC LARD SOAP

This soap is colored with cocoa and scented with (artificial) chocolate and vanilla fragrance oils. Although some of the color fades when the soap dries, don't overdo it with the cocoa, start with a rounded tablespoon and check the color.

Some people object to the use of animal products, but animal fat has been used in soap for centuries. In this recipe, the lard and the coconut oil together help make this a long-lasting bar. The weights in ounces are indicated in parentheses. *Remember, these are **weights**, not volumes.*

LARD	928 GRAMS (32.73 OZ.)
COCONUT OIL	702 GRAMS (24.76 OZ.)
OLIVE OIL	200 GRAMS (7.05 OZ.)
CANOLA OIL	702 GRAMS (24.76 OZ.)
LYE	12 OZ. DISSOLVED IN 700 GRAMS (24.7 OZ.) DISTILLED OR DEIONIZED WATER

SIMPLE NO-WEIGHING SOAP

A really simple recipe with commonly available ingredients; and it makes a very nice soap.

OK, so you don't have a scale and can't wait to start making soap. Well, here's a good beginner recipe that calls for oils and other ingredients you can find in the supermarket and health food store, and everything is measured, not weighed. To add your own touch, try adding about 1/2 cup of finely ground oatmeal or some kelp powder (green, a teaspoon or two for color) from your health food or bulk food store. When I made this, I added lily of the valley fragrance oil at light trace, before the soap got too thick. Simple, isn't it?

VEGETABLE SHORTENING	6 LBS. (COMMON SIZES ARE 3 AND 6 LB. CANS)
COCONUT OIL	14 FL. OZ. (FROM THE HEALTH FOOD STORE, USE THE WHOLE JAR)
OLIVE OIL	3/4 CUP
LYE	12 OZ. CAN DISSOLVED IN 2-3/4 CUP DISTILLED OR DEIONIZED WATER
LILY OF THE VALLEY FO	2 TBS. (OPTIONAL)

COTTONSEED OIL SOAP WITH LANOLIN

Often soap recipes have been developed at the request of friends. This recipe is in response to a challenge to see what sort of soap could be made using cottonseed oil. I wanted this to be a special hand soap, very moisturizing, so note the use of castor oil for increased lather, lanolin and jojoba oils as emollients, and just a touch of beeswax (mostly used to accelerate saponification). The weights in ounces are indicated in parentheses. *Remember, these are **weights**, not volumes.*

I had planned to make a blueberry scented soap but the blue color tab I used turned rather beige, so I added a hint of violet color tab and left it unscented. A nice hand soap, though, with the pumice.

OLIVE OIL	300 GRAMS (10.58 OZ.)
COTTONSEED OIL	226 GRAMS (7.97 OZ.)
JOJOBA OIL	45 GRAMS (1.59 OZ.)
PALM OIL	320 GRAMS (11.29 OZ.)
COCONUT OIL	625 GRAMS (22.05 OZ.)
CASTOR OIL	100 GRAMS (3.53 OZ.)
CANOLA OIL	650 GRAMS (22.93 OZ.)
BEESWAX	5 GRAMS (0.18 OZ.)
LANOLIN	25 GRAMS (0.88 OZ.)
LYE	12 OZ. DISSOLVED IN 700 GRAMS (24.7 OZ.) DISTILLED OR DEIONIZED WATER
PUMICE (OPTIONAL)	3/4 CUP

FAQ

HOW DO I MAKE BATH SALTS TO GO WITH MY SOAP?

Bath salts are pretty simple to make, and you have several choices. Basically, they are composed of one or more of epsom salts, sea salt, and baking soda. If baking soda is used, it is generally no more than about 1/3 of the total. Ideally, all components will have about the same particle size so you don't have big crystals of sea salt and fine powdered baking soda, since the fine stuff will tend to separate from the coarse over time. Once you have your blend of salts, add about a teaspoon of essential oil per pound and you have a nice fragrant bath salt.

TEA TREE OIL BAR

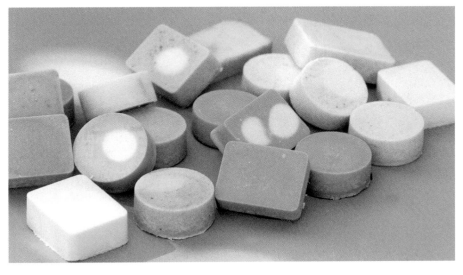

This is basically a white bar so I added some blue pigment to part of the batch and made white, blue, and variegated soap from the same batch. As you can see, pigments can give a nice intense color in a variety of shades.

A complex blend of vegetable oils, jojoba, aloe vera, and tea tree oil. Tea tree oil is noted for its antimicrobial, especially antifungal action; it is reportedly absorbed through the skin and can attack subdermal infections. Jojoba and aloe vera nourish the skin. This is a cleansing bar for problem skin areas - fungus, psoriasis, acne - as well as a great bath and shower bar. With its rich creamy lather, it works very well as a shampoo. The tea tree oil and aloe vera gel are added at trace. The weights in ounces are indicated in parentheses. *Remember, these are* **weights**, *not volumes.*

OLIVE OIL	175 GRAMS (6.17 OZ.)
JOJOBA OIL	50 GRAMS (1.76 OZ.)
PALM OIL	650 GRAMS (22.93 OZ.)
SOY OIL	650 GRAMS (22.93 OZ.)
CANOLA OIL	50 GRAMS (1.76 OZ.)
COCONUT OIL	660 GRAMS (23.28 OZ.)
TEA TREE OIL	25 GRAMS (0.88 OZ.)
ALOE VERA GEL	50 GRAMS (1.76 OZ.)
LYE	12 OZ. DISSOLVED IN 650 GRAMS (22.93 OZ.) DISTILLED OR DEIONIZED WATER

OATMEAL FACIAL BAR

The actual color of this bar depends on the amount of honey used and the temperature when the honey is added. The color at mixing is fairly dark but it lightens as it dries to a golden to nut brown color.

Finely ground oatmeal provides gentle abrasion to clear clogged pores and oily skin while jojoba and aloe vera replenish vital nutrients to keep skin clean, healthy, and supple. The unique beauty of this golden mottled bar can be enhanced by the addition of a pleasant touch of lavender essential oil. The weights in ounces are indicated in parentheses. *Remember, these are **weights**, not volumes.*

OLIVE OIL	160 GRAMS (5.64 OZ.)
SOY OIL	660 GRAMS (23.28 OZ.)
PALM OIL	660 GRAMS (23.28 OZ.)
CANOLA OIL	50 GRAMS (1.76 OZ.)
COCONUT OIL	665 GRAMS (23.46 OZ.)
JOJOBA OIL	30 GRAMS (1.06 OZ.)
OATMEAL, GROUND	3/4 CUP
LYE	12 OZ. DISSOLVED IN 700 GRAMS (24.7 OZ.) DISTILLED OR DEIONIZED WATER
LAVENDER OIL (OPTIONAL)	2-1/2 TSP.

LAVENDER GOAT'S MILK SOAP

No, this is not made with milk from lavender goats. It is a rich soap containing cocoa butter, jojoba oil, chamomile, powdered goat's milk, and lavender essential oil. Chamomile, of course, is noted for its healing powers and its rich herbal aroma blends subtly with the lavender. Use an electric food mill to pulverize the chamomile and blend it with the goat's milk solids. These are added, together with the essential oil, at trace; best mixed in with a stainless steel wire whisk. The weights in ounces are indicated in parentheses. *Remember, these are **weights**, not volumes.*

For this soap I put a slice of unscented pale green soap in the mold and then poured the goat milk soap over all to fill the mold.

CANOLA OIL	670 GRAMS (23.64 OZ.)
OLIVE OIL	180 GRAMS (6.35 OZ.)
PALM OIL	770 GRAMS (27.16 OZ.)
COCONUT OIL	720 GRAMS (25.40 OZ.)
JOJOBA OIL	20 GRAMS (0.71 OZ.)
COCOA BUTTER	25 GRAMS (0.88 OZ.)
LYE	12 OZ. DISSOLVED IN 600 GRAMS (21.2 OZ.) DISTILLED OR DEIONIZED WATER
POWDERED GOAT'S MILK	50 GRAMS (1.76 OZ.)
CHAMOMILE, GROUND	11 GRAMS (0.39 OZ.)
LAVENDER EO	2 TBS. (1 OZ.)

FAQ

I WANT TO MAKE ENOUGH LYE SOLUTION FOR SEVERAL BATCHES. CAN I STORE AND REHEAT LYE?

Certainly you can store and reheat lye, but first make sure no one will mistake the lye solution for ordinary water while it's being stored. Cover the lye solution with a lid or something like plastic wrap to keep it from air. You can reheat lye by placing it in a pan of warm water. I cannot recommend trying to heat it in a microwave, since it could easily boil over and give you a dangerous mess to clean up. Make sure that any glass or plastic item used to store and heat lye is in good shape, without cracks or chips.

MASQUE DE LIMONE

It is fairly simple to design a good moisturizing soap for dry skin, but I have often been asked for recommendations for oily skin as well. I finally decided to combine several approaches to loosen and remove excess skin oils, replacing them with just a touch of mild jojoba. This lemony bar is the first I have made using the cold process that does not rapidly lose its fresh, lemony scent. Again, an electric food mill is used to pulverize the lemon peel and lemongrass, which are added at trace along with the clay, Vitamin E, and lemon extract. Be sure to add the Vitamin E before the ground herbs. The weights in ounces are indicated in parentheses. *Remember, these are **weights**, not volumes.*

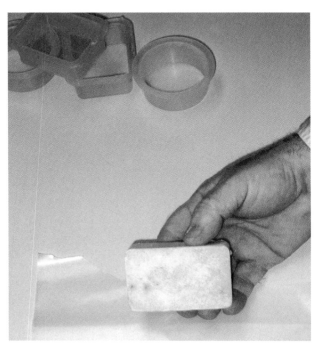

The lemon mask has an interesting color all by itself. As this picture shows, the aged soap (in hand) is lighter than that freshly made and uncured.

OLIVE OIL	303 GRAMS (10.69 OZ.)
CANOLA OIL	1320 GRAMS (46.56 OZ.)
PALM OIL	1550 GRAMS (54.67 OZ.)
COCONUT OIL	1460 GRAMS (51.50 OZ.)
JOJOBA OIL	14 GRAMS (.50 OZ.)
LYE	24 OZ. DISSOLVED IN 1300 GRAMS (45.9 OZ.) DISTILLED OR DEIONIZED WATER
VITAMIN E	0.5 OZ.
LEMON PEEL, DRIED	40 GRAMS (1.41 OZ.)
LEMONGRASS	10 GRAMS (0.35 OZ.)
FRENCH CLAY	3/4 CUP
6X LEMON EXTRACT	2 TBS (1 OZ.)

MENTHOL MINT SHAVING SOAP

A little yellow color tab gives a pleasant pale yellow to this minty bar.

This could actually be called a chocolate mint soap, since the cocoa butter brings that lovely chocolate scent through along with the mint. Smells good enough to eat and contains a special blend of ingredients to boost the lather and lubricate and cool the skin. It was designed for a high altitude army parachutist who needed a very close shave to fit his breathing equipment precisely to his face. The weights in ounces are indicated in parentheses. *Remember, these are **weights**, not volumes.*

COCOA BUTTER	50 GRAMS (1.76 OZ.)
SHEA BUTTER	50 GRAMS (1.76 OZ.)
BEESWAX	5 GRAMS (0.18 OZ.)
CASTOR OIL	200 GRAMS (7.05 OZ.)
OLIVE OIL	200 GRAMS (7.05 OZ.)
COCONUT OIL	650 GRAMS (22.93 OZ.)
CANOLA OIL	400 GRAMS (14.11 OZ.)
PALM OIL	670 GRAMS (23.64 OZ.)
GLYCERIN	50 GRAMS (1.76 OZ.)
LYE	12 OZ. DISSOLVED IN 700 GRAMS (24.7 OZ.) DISTILLED OR DEIONIZED WATER

AT TRACE, ADD:

CLAY	100 GRAMS (3.53 OZ.)
STEARIC ACID	20 GRAMS (0.71 OZ.)
MENTHOL	10 GRAMS (0.35 OZ.)
CAMPHOR EO	1 TSP.

LAVENDER SHAMPOO/CONDITIONER BAR

Castor oil is added, together with an additional amount of glycerin, to boost and stabilize the lather. A generous amount of jojoba oil is added to provide conditioning from the fatty alcohol byproduct of saponification. *Note:* This soap can get quite thick but may resist solidification, so stir to heavy trace before molding and wait until it is quite solid before you remove it from the molds. It is worth the extra effort. The weights in ounces are indicated in parentheses. *Remember, these are* **weights***, not volumes.*

This three layer soap was made using shocking pink, yellow, and green color tabs. Just divide the batch into three parts, mix the colors, and pour it in layers.

CASTOR OIL	330 GRAMS (11.64 OZ.)
COCONUT OIL	650 GRAMS (22.93 OZ.)
OLIVE OIL	600 GRAMS (21.16 OZ.)
JOJOBA OIL	200 GRAMS (7.05 OZ.)
CANOLA OIL	550 GRAMS (19.40 OZ.)
GLYCERIN	50 GRAMS (1.76 OZ.)
LYE	12 OZ. DISSOLVED IN 650 GRAMS (22.93 OZ.) DISTILLED OR DEIONIZED WATER
LAVENDER EO	1 TBS. (1/2 OZ.) AT TRACE

FAQ

WILL CASTOR OIL MAKE MY SOAP LATHER BETTER?

Many people ask about adding castor oil to soap to improve the amount of lather. Castor oil itself does not add to the amount of lather, only the soap made from castor oil is effective. So to achieve full effect, castor oil should be present at the start of saponification, not added at trace as to superfat.

ROYAL CASTILE SOAP

By itself, this bar is pure white, but for visual effect it is nice to divide the batch into portions, and make layered soaps. Shown are layers colored with kelp, cocoa, and paprika.

This soap resulted from a challenge to produce a rich olive oil heavy Castile soap without waiting days for it to solidify. So, starting with olive oil, I added coconut to boost the lather, then added jojoba oil to counteract the defatting nature of the coconut oil component. The result has a wonderful texture and full floral scent from the essential oils that are added at trace. The weights in ounces are indicated in parentheses. *Remember, these are* **weights**, *not volumes.*

OLIVE OIL	1800 GRAMS (63.50 OZ.)
COCONUT OIL	500 GRAMS (17.64 OZ.)
JOJOBA OIL	30 GRAMS (1.06 OZ.)
LYE	12 OZ. DISSOLVED IN 700 GRAMS (24.7 OZ.) DISTILLED OR DEIONIZED WATER
YLANG-YLANG 2 EO	2 TSP.
LAVENDER EO	1 TSP.
PALMAROSA EO	1/2 TSP.
ROSEMARY EO	1/2 TSP.

CLEOPATRA'S BEAUTY BAR

A nice soap for a varied color touch with a pale green (color tab) slice imbedded in a shocking pink base. A nice combination with strawberry fragrance oil.

An alternate color approach with a touch of blue color tab for a very pale blue tint.

Various legends say that Cleopatra's famous beauty was preserved by frequent baths in mare's or ass's milk. Since those are a bit hard to find these days, I substituted nonfat dry milk solids and included shea butter and honey, with just a touch of beeswax. Milk solids and honey are added at trace. Always avoid adding too much honey, since it tends to make a sticky soap. The weights in ounces are indicated in parentheses. *Remember, these are* **weights**, *not volumes.*

OLIVE OIL	150 GRAMS (5.29 OZ.)
CANOLA OIL	650 GRAMS (22.93 OZ.)
COCONUT OIL	725 GRAMS (25.57 OZ.)
PALM OIL	775 GRAMS (27.34 OZ.)
SHEA BUTTER	15 GRAMS (0.53 OZ.)
BEESWAX	5 GRAMS (0.18 OZ.)
LYE	12 OZ. DISSOLVED IN 700 GRAMS (24.7 OZ.) DISTILLED OR DEIONIZED WATER
MILK SOLIDS	30 GRAMS (1.06 OZ.)
HONEY	20 GRAMS (0.71 OZ.)

DR. BOB'S FACIAL SOAP

This soap naturally is a light brown, like an oatmeal cookie, so it is a good candidate for a little cocoa for a darker tint. For optimum effect, try imbedding a pistachio-colored slice.

Although there is no extra essential or fragrance oil added to this bar, it does tend to smell like an oatmeal cookie when warm. This is a very mild chamomile soap with ground oatmeal to exfoliate dead skin cells. At trace, the oatmeal and chamomile are added and when they are completely combined, the honey is added. The oatmeal is an ideal additive to counteract the tendency of honey to produce a sticky, hard to solidify bar. The weights in ounces are indicated in parentheses. *Remember, these are* **weights**, *not volumes.*

OLIVE OIL	300 GRAMS (10.58 OZ.)
COCONUT OIL	1450 GRAMS (51.15 OZ.)
PALM OIL	1550 GRAMS (54.67 OZ.)
CANOLA OIL	1310 GRAMS (46.21 OZ.)
JOJOBA OIL	15 GRAMS (0.53 OZ.)
SHEA BUTTER	20 GRAMS (0.71 OZ.)
LYE	24 OZ. DISSOLVED IN 1400 GRAMS (39.4 OZ.) DISTILLED OR DEIONIZED WATER
OATMEAL	1-1/2 CUPS FINELY GROUND, PREFERABLY REGULAR, NOT INSTANT
CHAMOMILE	20 GRAMS (0.71 OZ.) FINELY GROUND
HONEY	45 GRAMS (1.59 OZ.)

DR. BOB'S FEEL GOOD SOAP

Dr. Bob's Feel Good Herbal Soap. The addition of kelp helps give a pronounced herbal green.

My signature herbal soap, made with herbs and essential oils with a long history of use in herbal medicine to treat various skin insults and injuries. The trick to this bar is adding the Vitamin E at trace, before the ground herbs are added, in order to preserve a greenish tint to the bars, which can be enhanced by the addition of chlorophyll or, in this case, powdered kelp. As usual, the aloe vera gel is added at trace. Note that the addition of the Vitamin E after the herbs generally produces a brown bar. The weights in ounces are indicated in parentheses. *Remember, these are **weights**, not volumes.*

OLIVE OIL	300 GRAMS (10.58 OZ.)
COCONUT OIL	1460 GRAMS (51.50 OZ.)
PALM OIL	1560 GRAMS (55.03 OZ.)
CANOLA OIL	1305 GRAMS (46.03 OZ.)
JOJOBA OIL	37 GRAMS (1.31 OZ.)
LYE	24 OZ. DISSOLVED IN 1250 GRAMS (44.1 OZ.) DISTILLED OR DEIONIZED WATER
VITAMIN E	2 TBS. (1 OZ.)
ALOE VERA GEL	100 GRAMS (3.53 OZ.)
CHAMOMILE	19 GRAMS (0.67 OZ.)
COMFREY	18 GRAMS (0.63 OZ.)
HYSSOP	17 GRAMS (0.60 OZ.)
HOPS	14 GRAMS (0.49 OZ.)
FEVERFEW	18 GRAMS (0.63 OZ.)
LAVENDER FLOWERS	27 GRAMS (0.95 OZ.)
KELP POWDER	2 TBS. (1 OZ.)
LAVENDER EO	2 TBS. (1 OZ.)
ROSEMARY EO	1 TBS. (1/2 OZ.)

FAQ

HOW DO I MAKE LAUNDRY SOAP?

In the past, laundry soaps often came in bar form. These bars were usually a mixture of soap and 50% washing soda (sodium carbonate, not baking soda, which is sodium bicarbonate). Laundry soaps that were yellow also contained rosin, probably 1% to 2% of the bar. Since laundry soaps didn't need to be formulated to do anything other than clean clothing, they usually were made from coconut oil (for suds) and tallow. Although today you could add sodium carbonate to your soap at trace, it would really be easier to make a simple soap, grate it, and add washing soda to the wash water separately. Add the grated soap to the wash water and let it dissolve before adding clothes to avoid creating a gummy mess (undissolved soap) on your clothing.

AVOCADO GREEN SOAP

Pigments come in shades as well as colors, hence the distinct difference in these bars using two different green pigments. The third bar is the result of pouring green cold process soap on top of a red melt and pour layer. Let the melt and pour layer completely solidify before pouring the warm cold process soap on top.

This recipe springs from the skin nourishing properties of avocado kernel oil. The amount shown, 200 grams, can be increased to 250 grams for a little additional superfatting for dry skin. Although the recipe is written using shortening, lard may be substituted on an equal weight basis. Lemongrass and kelp (which are added at trace) are considered skin nourishing as well as giving a nice green color to the bar. *Remember, these are **weights**, not volumes.*

SHORTENING	900 GRAMS (31.75 OZ.)
OLIVE OIL	500 GRAMS (17.64 OZ.)
COCONUT OIL	700 GRAMS (24.69 OZ.)
AVOCADO KERNEL	200 GRAMS (7.05 OZ.)
LYE	12 OZ. DISSOLVED IN 700 GRAMS (24.7 OZ.) DISTILLED OR DEIONIZED WATER
LAVENDER EO	1 TBS.
ROSEMARY EO	1 TSP.
VETIVER EO	1/2 TSP.
LEMONGRASS	2 TBS. FINELY GROUND HERB OR 1/2 TSP. EO
KELP	3 TBS. POWDER

Corn Oil Soap

This bar started with a melt and pour layer colored with a gold pearlescent pigment. When this solidified, the cold process soap, with a brick red pigment for color, was added to fill the mold.

Many common oils found in the grocery will make a nice bar of soap. Here is one where corn oil has replaced the olive oil. Add scent and color as desired. *Remember, these are **weights**, not volumes.*

CORN OIL	600 GRAMS (21.16 OZ.)
CASTOR OIL	200 GRAMS (7.05 OZ.)
COCONUT OIL	600 GRAMS (21.16 OZ.)
PALM OIL	900 GRAMS (31.75 OZ.)
LYE	12 OZ. DISSOLVED IN 700 GRAMS (24.7 OZ.) DISTILLED OR DEIONIZED WATER

APRICOT SOAP

This bar was colored with a deep yellow pigment to emphasize the apricot theme. The color is not unlike that produced by turmeric, just a little more intense.

This recipe has quite a bit of flexibility. Olive oil can be used in place of the canola on an equal weight basis, and the apricot kernel oil can be increased to 250 grams to add extra mildness (superfatting). A half ounce of Vitamin E can also be added at trace for an extra beneficial touch. To match the composition, turmeric is used to give a peachy color and a peach nectar fragrance oil is used for scent. *Remember, these are* **weights**, *not volumes.*

CANOLA OIL	500 GRAMS (17.64 OZ.)
COCONUT OIL	700 GRAMS (24.69 OZ.)
PALM OIL	900 GRAMS (31.75 OZ.)
APRICOT KERNEL OIL	200 GRAMS (7.05 OZ.)
LYE	12 OZ. DISSOLVED IN 700 GRAMS (24.7 OZ.) DISTILLED OR DEIONIZED WATER
TURMERIC	1 TO 2 TBS.
PEACH FO	1-1/2 OZ.
VITAMIN E	1/2 OZ. (OPTIONAL)

ABILENE TRAIL SOAP

The Abilene Trail, of course, was a major route for transporting cattle from the Southwest to market. This recipe, then, is for those of you who take the time and effort to process your own tallow, as well as those lucky ones who are able to buy refined tallow. It makes a fine hard bar to which can be added, for extra mildness, a bit of jojoba oil as additional superfat. Sandalwood, essential or fragrance oil, is a nice touch for the trail boss. *Remember, these are* **weights**, *not volumes.*

This is a simple layered color effect, using only cold process soap with pigments. In this case, a natural or uncolored base (about half the batch) was poured into the molds and the remainder of the batch was colored with a red pigment and then poured on top of the first layer. If you don't want mixing, the original layer must be thick enough to completely support the subsequent layers.

TALLOW	750 GRAMS (26.46 OZ.)
OLIVE OIL	950 GRAMS (33.51 OZ.)
COCONUT OIL	600 GRAMS (21.16 OZ.)
JOJOBA OIL	50 GRAMS (OPTIONAL)
LYE	12 OZ. DISSOLVED IN 700 GRAMS (24.7 OZ.) DISTILLED OR DEIONIZED WATER
SANDALWOOD EO	1 OZ. (1-1/2 TO 2 OZ. FRAGRANCE OIL MAY BE SUBSTITUTED)

SUNNY DAY SOAP

This is a nicely (almost 5%) superfatted soap that contains jojoba, sunflowerseed oil, and Vitamin E in addition to palm, olive, and coconut oils. Add scent and color to please. *Remember, these are* **weights***, not volumes.*

This sunrise effect came from using a natural base at full, thick trace, with some red pigment soap poured on top. In this case, after the red top layer was poured, I used a knife to swirl the colored layer into the plain base. If you use longer molds, you can create a marbled effect by pouring a thick colored layer into a channel on the surface and then using the knife to create color swirls.

COCONUT OIL	675 GRAMS (23.81 OZ.)
OLIVE OIL	500 GRAMS (17.64 OZ.)
PALM OIL	800 GRAMS (28.22 OZ.)
JOJOBA OIL	100 GRAMS (3.53 OZ.)
SUNFLOWERSEED OIL	300 GRAMS (10.58 OZ.)
LYE	12 OZ. DISSOLVED IN 650 GRAMS (22.93 OZ.) DISTILLED OR DEIONIZED WATER
VITAMIN E	1/2 OZ. ADDED AT TRACE

LUSCIOUS LUXURY BAR

This is a very special moisturizing soap containing jojoba oil, lanolin, lots of olive oil, Vitamin E for a special skin treat, and a bit of beeswax to keep it long lasting (and speed up the time to trace) as well as luxurious. Since some people are allergic to lanolin, be sure that you label the lanolin content. For an extra special touch, add a bit of aloe vera gel and finely ground chamomile flowers at trace. *Remember, these are* **weights**, *not volumes.*

This is another example of a hybrid between melt and pour and cold process soap. This time I started with a thin layer of melt and pour soap colored with a gold mica pigment, then added the yellow pigmented cold process soap layer.

COCONUT OIL	600 GRAMS (21.16 OZ.)
OLIVE OIL	875 GRAMS (30.86 OZ.)
JOJOBA OIL	100 GRAMS (3.53 OZ.)
PALM OIL	750 GRAMS (26.46 OZ.)
BEESWAX	25 GRAMS (0.88 OZ.)
LANOLIN	50 GRAMS (1.76 OZ.)
LYE	12 OZ. DISSOLVED IN 650 GRAMS (22.93 OZ.) DISTILLED OR DEIONIZED WATER.
VITAMIN E	1/2 OZ. ADDED AT TRACE

PET SHAMPOO BAR

Sure, dogs don't really care what color the soap is: a bath will still be an insult to their dignity. However, here are two pigmented colors for Mama - a nice lavender and a plum, which come from pigments. Pigments offer the soapmaker the ability to produce rich vibrant colors.

This is a favorite recipe of my Shepherd, especially good after a long weekend at puppy camp (dog kennel) when he needs a little extra tender loving care. It is very mild, with only about 21% coconut oil; enough to generate lather but not enough to be especially drying. The shortening is the all vegetable type. Manuka essential oil can be substituted for the tea tree oil and lemon balm (melissa) for the clary sage. The aloe vera gel, Vitamin E, ground chamomile, and essential oils are added at trace. *Remember, these are **weights**, not volumes.*

CASTOR OIL	100 GRAMS (3.53 OZ.)
COCONUT OIL	500 GRAMS (17.64 OZ.)
OLIVE OIL	250 GRAMS (8.82 OZ.)
PALM OIL	500 GRAMS (17.64 OZ.)
SHORTENING	1000 GRAMS (35.27 OZ.)
LYE	12 OZ. DISSOLVED IN 650 GRAMS (22.9 OZ.) DISTILLED OR DEIONIZED WATER
LAVENDER EO	1 TBS.
TEA TREE EO	2 TBS. (1 OZ.)
ROSEMARY EO	1 TSP.
CLARY SAGE EO	1/2 TSP.
VITAMIN E	1/2 OZ.

PET SHAMPOO II

For Mama again, here are blue and green pigmented bars. The green was made from the same batch, separating a small amount for a separate color treatment and drizzling it over the top of the blue soap. Since the bottom of the mold yields a smoother soap than the open top, the added color layer ends up on the bottom of the finished bar.

If anything, this recipe is even slightly milder than the first Pet Shampoo Bar, but the essential oil blend (lavender, eucalyptus, cypress, and citronella) is selected for its insect repellent properties. You can also add pennyroyal and lemongrass or use them to replace, at equal amounts, the citronella and cypress. This might be a good soap to use on a pet who is about to go to puppy camp or who is going to spend some time with you camping. Remember, these are **weights**, not volumes.

COCONUT OIL	500 GRAMS (17.64 OZ.)
OLIVE OIL	350 GRAMS (12.35 OZ.)
PALM OIL	600 GRAMS (21.16 OZ.)
SHORTENING	900 GRAMS (31.75 OZ.)
LYE	12 OZ. DISSOLVED IN 700 GRAMS (24.7 OZ.) DISTILLED OR DEIONIZED WATER
LAVENDER EO	3 TSP.
EUCALYPTUS EO	1 TSP.
CYPRESS EO	1/2 TSP.
CITRONELLA EO	1/2 TSP.

A Few Thoughts on Yield

By this time you are probably starting to wonder, "But how many molds do I need?" or perhaps, "How much soap will that recipe actually make?" The simplistic answer, of course, is that it depends on the type of molds you are using. That information, however, is not particularly helpful, especially when you have a pot of soap that is starting to get thick and you are suddenly wondering where you are going to put it all. So here are a few guiding thoughts about molds and volume.

When I make soap I ordinarily use 2-1/2 to 4 fluid ounce plastic molds. The number of bars of soap depends on how many 2-1/2 ounce molds I use compared to how many 4 ounce molds, but in general, my recipes that use 24 ounces of lye (by weight) generally yield about 55 to 60 bars of soap, which weigh a total of approximately 15 pounds. Recipes that call for added solids such as ground oatmeal or pumice make a few more bars than those without.

For those of you who chose PVC pipe molds, an 18" piece of 3" inner diameter pipe has an inner volume of roughly 70 fluid ounces. This means that it would take two full 18" sections of pipe mold to contain the recipe I mentioned above.

If you have a rectangular plastic container or stainless steel baking pan with dimensions of 10" by 16" by 2", the contained volume is roughly 177 fluid ounces (not enough volume for this recipe, which can produce up to 240 fluid ounces of raw soap).

Some of you, of course, will intend to enter the commercial realm of soapmaking. That is, you will one day start to sell the soap you make. (I mean you can only use or give away so much and soapmaking is addictive!) For commercial enterprises, though, weight is generally the important factor, not volume. In this case you will be concerned about calculating the yield of these recipes in terms of weight of soap that it will produce.

If you want to determine how much soap your recipe will make, try this method. It's based on the theory that the total raw soap produced is simply the sum of the weights of all the ingredients: oils, lye, water, fragrance materials, and other additives. Weigh everything, add it up, and that is what you will get out of the pot and into your mold. Of course, the curing process is also a drying process and as the soap cures and ages, it dries out and shrinks slightly. There is no simple way to predict the cured weight of a one pound or half kilogram chunk of fresh soap. The only volatile materials (which can evaporate and lower the weight of the finished soap) are the water and fragrance oils you added, so an extreme estimate of the final yield of soap would be the sum of the ingredients except for the water you added with the lye. In reality, you will not lose all of this water; half to two thirds is more typical. (The amount you actually lose will depend on the humidity and temperature where you cure the soap, and length of time of curing.)

FAQ

I found a recipe I want to try, but it is too large. What do I do?

In general, recipes can be scaled up or down with few problems. If you cut all amounts in the recipe by half (all amounts, lye, water, and oils), the proportions will still be good. When you are decreasing the size of a recipe, you will frequently need to increase the temperatures of the oils by five or so degrees and when you increase the size you should decrease the temperatures by the same five degrees. This allows for an increase or decrease in the rate at which heat is lost during your soapmaking.

CHAPTER 12

ALTERNATIVE OILS AND HOW TO USE THEM

Although the most commonly used soap oils are olive, coconut, and palm, together with lard and vegetable shortening, many oils can be used either in the basic recipe or to add as a superfat, extra moisturizing oil, at trace. One of the questions most frequently asked by new soapmkaers is, "Can I substitute oil X for Y." The answer to that questions is that oils with the same SAP (saponifcation value, see page 116) can be totally or partially substituted in a recipe on a one-to-one weight basis.

More importantly, as you gain expertise, you will want to create your own recipes. Perhaps you have found a really nice oil that you think will make good soap, or perhaps you want to limit the oils you use to two - and I haven't included a recipe that suits your taste.

Whatever your reason, it is fairly simple to create your own recipe. The amount of lye required to make soap is calculated from the Saponification Value or Sap Value, usually abbreviated as SAP or S.V. The SAP is chemically defined as the number of milligrams of potassium hydroxide required to completely hydrolyze (saponify) one gram of oil. However, most tables assembled for soapmaking, mine included, report the SAP as the number of grams of sodium or potassium hydroxide needed to neutralize one gram of oil. Thus, if you know the SAP for the oils you will use and the number of grams of oil, it is easy to calculate the number of grams of lye needed. The general approach to the calculations are:

A. Weigh out the oils you plan to use. For example:

Coconut oil	200 grams
Soybean oil	300 grams
Olive oil	250 grams

Look up the SAP from the table on page 116

Coconut	.191
Soybean	.136
Olive	.135

B. Multiply the weight of each oil by its SAP to find the amount of lye needed for that oil.

Coconut oil	200 x .191 = 38.2 grams lye
Soybean	300 x .136 = 40.8 grams lye
Olive	250 x .135 = 33.8 grams lye

C. Add the amount of lye used by all the oils. 38.2 + 40.8 + 33.8 = 112.8 grams lye

D. To calculate the amount of distilled water needed (the lye should be under 40% of the total) divide 112.8 by .4 = 282 grams water.

If you are measuring the weight of oil in ounces, the steps are exactly the same and the result is ounces of lye needed instead of grams.

Although an oil, coconut oil (shown being weighed) is a low melting solid.

The following list describes most oils available to, asked about, and used by soapmakers. Remember that "unsaponifiables" are generally considered emollients (skin softeners), which are mainly composed of tocopherols (natural forms of Vitamin E) and sterols; unsaponifiables help preserve and promote the natural elastic properties of skin.

Lauric and myristic acids are mainly responsible for producing high levels of lather, though are harsher than the longer chain fatty acids such as oleic acid, the primary constituent of olive oil. High levels of linoleic and especially linolenic acid generally produce a tendency to turn rancid both in the soap (when stored in hot humid conditions) and in the oil itself, and so should ordinarily be used with some form of antioxidant. When used in superfatting soap, howev-er, oils with high levels of linoleic and linolenic acids are thought to penetrate the skin easily with a resulting skin softening effect; for this reason these oils are often used in bath oil and skin care cosmetic formulations.

ALMOND OIL (Amygdalus communis, "sweet almond" oil). In Greek mythology, Phyllis was left behind when Demophon, son of Theseus, went to war. She committed suicide and was turned into an almond tree. Upon his return, the crying Demophon hugged the tree and it blossomed for the first time. Almond oil is a yellow oil with slight characteristic odor. Widespread use in cosmetic products, soap, and makeup. Contains mostly oleic and linoleic acids, and up to 1.2% unsaponifiables.

APRICOT KERNEL OIL (Prunus Armeniaca). Straw colored oily liquid. Contains mostly oleic and linoleic acids; has high emollient properties and is often used in bath oils.

AVOCADO SEED OIL (Persia Americana). Colorless oily liquid, bland odor. It is an important source of unsaponifiables, containing 2% to 11% unsaponifiables. Oil readily penetrates skin and is used both as an emollient and to retard moisture loss. Used in hair, hand, and face products.

BABASSU OIL (Orbygnia oleifera). Light yellow semi-solid that typically contains 50% lauric, 20% myristic acids. Where it's readily available, it's often used as a substitute for coconut or palm kernel oil to produce strong persistent lather. Used in cos-metics to retard moisture loss in skin, and is sometimes used to combat stretch marks.

BEESWAX. Yellowish to brownish-yellow, soft to brittle, honey-like odor, balsamic taste. Consists of "wax" esters (that is, without glycerin) of very long chain fatty alcohols and fatty acids. Also contains about 20% hydrocarbons. The melting point is from 62°C to 65°C (144°F to 149°F).

BORAGE SEED OIL (Borago officinalis). Pale yellow oil used in skin and hair care products, high (up to 40%) in linoleic acid and 20% to 25% gamma linolenic acid (GLA), an "essential fatty acid." Fights skin dehydration and loss of elasticity.

CANOLA OIL (genetic cultivars of brassica napus and rapa, also called lear oil, from low erucic acid rapeseed). Pale yellow bland edible oil. Low in saturated fatty acids (ca. 6%), canola has an oleic acid content nearly that of olive oil. It also contains omega-3 fatty acids, so-called Essential Fatty Acids. The original seed crop, rapeseed, has been cultivated at least since 2000 BC. Tocopherol content from 0.5% to 1%.

CASTOR OIL (Ricinus communis). Also known as Palma Christi Oil. Pale yellow, viscous oil derived from cold-pressing seeds. Excellent keeping properties; does not turn rancid unless heated excessively. Slightly acrid taste with nauseating aftertaste. Excellent ability to wet pigments, hence often used in lipsticks. Approximately 87% ricinoleic acid. Hydrogenated castor oil is sometimes available. In this case, the melting point is typically 84°C to 89°C (183°F to 192°F). Sulfated castor oil comes from reacting castor oil with a form of sulfuric acid; it is a semi-synthetic anionic surfactant and should not be used as a base stock for soap.

COCOA BUTTER (Theobroma cacao). Slightly yellow solid, consists of glycerides of stearic, palmitic, oleic, arachidic, and linoleic acids. Characteristic odor and taste of chocolate. Cosmetic uses in skin care products including bath oils. Solidifies at 21.5°C to 23°C (71°F to 73°F).

COCONUT OIL (Cocos nucifera). White semi-solid lard-like fat, stable to air, expressed from the kernels of the coconut palm. The melting point is 21°C to 25°C (70°F to 77°F). This is also called 76 degree coconut oil. Do not confuse with fractionated coconut oil, which is a liquid at room temperature and which is used primarily in lotions and toiletries, not in soap. Hydrogenated, or 92 degree coconut oil, is also available and may be used for soapmaking.

CORN OIL (Zea mays). Pale yellow bland oil; contains about 50% linoleic acid and 30% oleic acid, 1% to 2% unsaponifiables. Used in hand creams, lip balms, and massage oils.

COTTONSEED OIL (Gossypium herbaceum). Pale yellow oil, practically odorless fixed oil from seeds. Composition is very similar to soybean oil. There are many rumors suggesting that heavy pesticide use imparts a risk to the use of cottonseed oil; however, federal regulations severely restrict pesticide levels in all food grade oils available in the U.S., no matter if the oil is domestic or imported. Thus the risk should be no greater than for any oil seed except perhaps for organically grown crops.

EMU OIL. Fairly new to the market, these birds are being raised in the U.S. for meat and fat. The high quality odorless fat is high in linolenic acid and is reportedly used effectively to treat eczema, scarring, burns, psoriasis, and in general for skin and hair care. Contains approx. 47% oleic, 24% palmitic acids.

EVENING PRIMROSE OIL (Oenothera biennis). This native North American plant oil contains high amounts of linolenic acid, about 9% to 10%, with up to 80% linoleic. Used in moisturizing creams for face and hands and in lip balms. This is a popular additive in skin care formulations with some reported success in treating psoriasis.

FLAXSEED OIL (Linum usitatissimum). Better known as linseed oil, it is a yellow to light brown oil with an aroma reminiscent of butter. The Latin name refers to the ancient uses of linen which comes from the plant fiber. It is high in linoleic and linolenic acids and is rich in Vitamin E. However, it is still prone to turning rancid.

GRAPE SEED OIL (Vitis vinifera). Light greenish odorless oil. Rich in linoleic acid (almost 70%) and is used in skin and especially hair care products and shaving oils. The unsaponifiables contain appreciable amounts of tocopherols and sterols.

HAZELNUT OIL (Corylus avellana). The genus name "corylus" is Latin for helmet, which describes the fruit's shape. This is a light oil with a delicate aroma. Offers excellent skin penetrating ability and is used in skin and hair care products and lip balms.

HEMPSEED OIL (Cannabis sativa). Greenish color oil. Contains linoleic acid 50% plus 30% of linolenic acids, plus 1% to 1.3% unsaponifiables. Highly prone to oxidation, though refined oils are reported to be more stable.

JOJOBA OIL (Simmondsia chinensis and californica). A liquid wax ester extracted from seeds. Contains wax esters of unsaturated fatty alcohols and unsaturated fatty acids. Highly stable, can be stored for years without rancidity.

KUKUI OIL (Aleurites moluccana). Pale yellow oil with characteristic odor; used in skin and hair products. Contains 42% linoleic, 29% linolenic acids.

LARD. Purified internal fat from the abdomen of the hog. Soft white solid at room temperature. Contains mostly oleic, stearic, and palmitic acids. Used in soap and for ointments where absorption is desired.

MACADAMIA NUT OIL (Macadamia ternifolia). Pale yellow, odorless oil. It is a good penetrating oil that leaves a velvety feel to the skin. Resembles mink oil in composition and function. Used for skin care and makeup preparations. Rich in oleic (60%) and palmitoleic (20%) acids.

MANGO KERNEL OIL (Mangifera indica). Sometimes called mango butter, it is a yellowish solid rich in unsaponifiables (1% to 5%). It is mostly comprised of stearic, oleic, and palmitic acids. Used in hand creams and overnight cremes.

MINK OIL (from pelts of Mustela). Used in bath oils and hair care products, leaves a nongreasy velvety finish on skin. Rich in oleic acid and resembles macadamia nut oil in composition and function.

OLIVE OIL (Olea europaea). A pale yellow to greenish-yellow fixed oil obtained by expression from the ripe olives using hydraulic presses. Becomes rancid on exposure to air. Produces a mild soap that is enriched by its unsaponifiable content. It has limited use in cosmetics since it may impart a tacky feeling to skin. High oleic acid content, unsaponifiables 0.5% to 1.5%.

OLIVE POMACE OIL. A greenish liquid obtained by solvent extraction of the residue from several pressings. Rich in unsaponifiables, this oil is generally blended with virgin olive oil to meet industry standards for free fatty acid and taste. Generally higher in peroxides and thus possibly less stable than virgin grades. Not to be confused with pomace oil from grape seed which is also frequently blended with minor amounts (ca. 10%) of olive oil.

PALM OIL refined (Elaeis guineensis). Reddish yellow to pale yellow fatty mass with faint odor of violet. This is often used in soap formulations to produce a harder, longer lasting bar; chemically and physically it is quite similar to lard. In cosmetics it is used as an occlusive agent in skin care and bath formulations.

PALM KERNEL OIL (Elaeis quineensis). Pale yellow to white solid. Depending on locale, this may be either more available or less expensive than coconut oil, which is its functional equivalent in soapmaking.

SAFFLOWER OIL (Carthamus tinctorius). Oil from the milled and extracted seeds. Edible drying oil intermediate between soy and linseed. Less than 1.5% unsaponifiables. Thickens and becomes rancid on prolonged exposure to air but stabilized it is used in skin and hair conditioning products.

SESAME SEED OIL (Sesamum indicum). Resistant to oxidation, used in skin conditioners and moisturizers, bath oils, and the like. One of the oldest cultivated plants (at least 4,000 years of cultivation). High in linoleic and oleic acids and contains unique natural antioxidants. Approximately 2% unsaponifiables.

SHEA BUTTER (Butyrospermum parkii, from the fruit of the African Karite tree). Pale yellow paste, melting between 35°C and 43°C (95°F to 109°F), with slight odor. Isolated from the nut of the African Karite tree. Contains up to 55% oleic acid and 40% stearic, with up to 17% unsaponifiables. Reported ability as a sun block comes from its natural trace content of cinnamic acid. Useful in cosmetics to retard moisture loss.

SOYBEAN OIL (Glycine max or soja). Pale yellow to brownish-yellow oil obtained from soybeans principally by extraction with hexane or heptane. Slight characteristic odor and taste. Used in hand creams and lip balms. Contains .5% to 1.5% unsaponifiables.

SUNFLOWER OIL (Helianthus annuus). Pale yellow oil with

Sunflowers of Minnesota

bland taste from the milled seeds. Vitamin E content approaches that of wheat germ oil. Often used in skin and hair products and bath oils.

TALLOW. Fat from bovine cattle and sheep. Tallow sometimes specifically refers to the hard fat found around the kidneys. It is one of the most used components of commercial soaps due to its mildness (as the soap), availability, and low cost.

WALNUT OIL (Juglans regia). Contains 55% to 65% linoleic acid and 0.5% to 1% unsaponifiables high in sitosterols. Often used in products to combat wrinkles around eyes and in hand creams for damaged skin. The name implies "Jove's acorn" and "royal" (since it was imported by Persian kings). The walnut itself symbolizes desire, marriage, and fecundity although the tree has held a generally sinister reputation, often associated with witches and witchcraft.

VEGETABLE SHORTENING. Exact compositions vary depending on manufacturer and country. Malaysian products are mostly fractionated palm oils; Canadian products are frequently based on canola, while many in the U.S. are either partially hydrogenated soybean oil blends (PHSBO) or blends of PHSBO with hardened cottonseed oil. Those blended with animal fat are called compound shortenings. Iodine values and SAP will vary, but an iodine value of 77 and a SAP of 192 are reasonable values for general purpose shortenings.

WHEAT GERM OIL (Triticum vulgare). Thick honey colored oil with a slight odor; good source of tocopherols and Vitamin A. Rich in sterols, 3% to 4% unsaponifiables. Wheat is an ancient crop whose "invention" or source as a gift from the gods is claimed by Egyptians, Greeks, and Romans. Used in hair and skin products, lip balms.

SAP VALUES FOR FATS, OILS, AND WAXES

WHAT IS KOH?

KOH is the chemical formula for potassium hydroxide, which is often used to make soft and liquid soaps. Since KOH is heavier than ordinary lye, the saponification value is different than that for sodium hydroxide.

I FINALLY FOUND A SOURCE OF POTASSIUM HYDROXIDE. HOW DO I USE IT TO MAKE SOAP?

Potassium hydroxide (KOH) is normally used to produce liquid soaps since potassium salts are much more water-soluble than sodium salts. The general procedure for use of potassium hydroxide is the same as for regular lye, but the proportions are different. Use the saponification values in the table on page 116 to calculate the amount of KOH to use and avoid any significant amount of superfatting since this will often produce a gel rather than a liquid. Concentrated potassium soaps are usually soft and often sticky compared to sodium soaps.

FAT OR OIL	SAP for Lye (NaOH)	INS	SAP for KOH
almond	0.139	97	0.196
apricot kernel	0.139	91	0.195
avocado kernel	0.133	99	0.186
babassu	0.175	230	0.245
castor	0.129	95	0.180
canola	0.124	56	0.174
cocoa	0.138	157	0.194
coconut	0.191	258	0.268
corn	0.137	69	0.192
cottonseed	0.139	89	0.194
flaxseed	0.135	-6	0.190
grapeseed	0.129	66	0.181
hempseed	0.137	39	0.193
jojoba	0.066	11	0.092
kukui	0.135	24	0.189
linseed	0.136	12	0.190
neem	0.139	124	0.195
olive	0.135	109	0.190
palm	0.142	145	0.199
palm kernel	0.157	183	0.220
peach kernel	0.137	96	0.192
peanut	0.137	99	0.192
safflower	0.137	47	0.192
sesame	0.134	81	0.188
shortening	0.137	115	0.192
shea butter	0.128	116	0.179
soybean	0.136	61	0.191
sunflower seed	0.135	63	0.189
wheat germ	0.131	58	0.183
carnauba wax	0.057	70	0.081
candelilla	0.042	n/a	0.060
beeswax	0.067	84	0.094
butterfat	0.162	191	0.227
chicken fat	0.142	130	0.199
deer fat	0.141	166	0.197
emu fat	0.137	128	0.193
goat fat	0.139	156	0.196
goat butter	0.167	n/a	0.235
goose fat	0.137	130	0.192
horse fat	0.141	117	0.198
lanolin	0.076	83	0.106
lard	0.141	139	0.198
mink oil	0.140	n/a	0.196
neat's foot	0.140	124	0.196
beef tallow	0.140	147	0.196
rabbit fat	0.143	116	0.201
sheep tallow	0.139	156	0.196
cod liver	0.128	29	0.180

CHAPTER 13
BEYOND COLD PROCESS SOAP

RE-MELTABLE AND TRANSLUCENT SOAPS

I do have some insights for those who wish to experiment with making re-meltable and translucent soaps, properties which often go hand in hand. For home use, there are some recipes published in the patent literature that can be easily searched on the Internet. Of course, you cannot sell these soaps since they are protected by patent law and those published may not be made using the ingredients you would like to use.

Some of the earliest translucent soaps were prepared from fatty acids using a mixture of sodium hydroxide and an organic base, triethanolamine or TEA (more chemical shorthand). The TEA amount was usually selected to neutralize about 25% of the fatty acids. This proportion produced a solid bar while the alcohol groups that are part of the TEA structure help to avoid excessive crystal formation and

it's the crystals that scatter light and produce opacity.

A second approach to true melt and pour soap was the use of neutral, but nonvolatile organic solvents such as propylene glycol or dipropylene glycol (not antifreeze, which is ethylene glycol and a poison). One or both solvents are usually incorporated into a sodium tallow-coconut soap blend at a level of 15% to 25% by weight. These bars are structurally similar to glass, which is termed a supercooled liquid. That is, they lack ordered crystalline structure but are much too viscous to flow unless heated. You may feel that the organic solvent makes the bar too harsh; but that is a judgment call.

New approaches to translucent and melt and pour soaps continue to develop. Although most are commercially produced directly from fatty acids, there does not appear to be a reason not to use cold processing to prepare them. The trick is to find the right combination of fats or oils, alkali, and additives to produce the desired effect of being readily re-meltable. Blends of coconut and tallow are ordinarily used, with the coconut being less than 20% of the total fatty acids. I have seen no reports of olive oil or other long chain oils being used to substitute for tallow, but that may be due to cost more than lack of functionality.

One often critical factor appears to be the type of alkali used to produce the soap. Recent patents mention the use of blends of sodium and potassium hydroxides, usually about 90% sodium hydroxide with the remainder potassium hydroxide. Potassium hydroxide is used to prepare liquid and soft soaps, so the blend seems to strike a balance between the tendency to liquefy and to form crystals that do not liquefy. The total amount of lye seems to be selected to exactly neutralize the fatty acids, that is, neither excess lye nor excess fat is desired, though it appears to be better to have a slight excess, typically 2% to 4%, of fatty acids which tends to prevent cracking of the bar as

well as improving lather and skin emolliency.

Most translucent and melt and pour soaps reported to date do contain additives to enhance clarity or melting properties. The additives include salts such as sodium chloride, potassium or sodium citrate or acetate (at .5% to 1% to inhibit formation of crystals on the surface when in contact with water), lanolin or lanolin fatty acids (at 1% to 2%), water (from 5% to 20%), and various amounts of polyols such as glycerin, propylene glycol, triethanolamine, sorbitol, polyethylene glycol, or sucrose.

Although they do not themselves promote transparency, fine silicas can be added to transparent bars without loss of clarity. Their function is to improve the character of the lather, controlling the bubble size.

Commercially, most additives are added to partially dried powdered soap at some modest elevated temperature to facilitate dissolving or formation of the proper crystal structure, called the beta phase. A double boiler, as used for rebatching, is probably the container of choice. Since the soap is ready-made, once you observe that the mixture has melted, it is time to quickly transfer it to a mold so that cooling can start at once.

About the Author

Photo by Sarah Johnson-Malchow.

Dr. McDaniel received a B. S. in Chemistry from the University of Notre Dame and a PhD in Organic Chemistry from the University of Missouri-Rolla. After almost two years as a Postdoctoral Fellow at the University of Chicago, he began his industrial career in the surfactant industry, developing the active ingredients that go into household detergents and fabric softeners. For the next 20 years he worked developing surfactants in various bench and management positions, earning 14 U.S. Patents along the way. In the late '80s he switched his professional focus to the paper industry; but, at the insistence of his wife Katie (weaver, fiber artist, chandler, and hot glass artist), he began making Dr. Bob's Herbal Soap at home as a craft. Dr. Bob also writes a special topics column for *The Saponifier* (a newspaper published for those interested in making soap and toiletries at home). He is listed in various recent editions *of Marquis Who's Who in America* and *Who's Who in Science and Engineering.*

Dr. Bob and Katie have one son, Ben, who is also a craftsman, a jeweler; he is currently serving as a U.S. Army Ranger.

Appendix

SUPPLIERS

Essential and Fragrance Oils

From Nature With Love
258 Longstreet Ave.
Bronx, NY 10465
Phone: (888) 376-6695
Fax: (718) 861-0669
kibbycbe@aol.com
www.from-nature-with-love.com
melt and pour soap and essential oils

Janca's Jojoba Oil Co.
456 East Juanita #7
Mesa, AZ 85204
Phone: (602) 497-9494
FAX: (602) 497-1312
essential and vegetable oils

Lavender Lane
7337 #1 Roseville Rd.
Sacramento, CA 95842
Phone: (916) 334-4400
bottles, jars, oils, cosmetics

The Lebermuth Co.
PO Box 4103
South Bend, IN 46634-4103
Phone: (800) 648-1123
Fax: (219) 258-7450
essential oils and extracts

Liberty Natural Products
SE Stark St.
Portland, OR 97215
Phone: (800) 289-8427 or (503) 256-1227
Fax: (503) 256-1182.
e-mail: liberty@teleport.com
essential and vegetable oils

Mint Meadow Country Oils
N 8573 Hwy H
Camp Douglas, WI 54618
Phone: (608) 427-3561
http://members.tripod.com/~mint meadow/index.html
e-mail: dshuman@mwt.net
peppermint and other mint oils

Nature's Gift Custom Aromatherapy
1040 Cheyenne Blvd.
Madison, TN 37115
Phone: (615) 612-4270
Fax: (615) 860-9171
www.naturesgift.com
essential oils

Rainbow Meadow
5234 Southern Blvd., Ste. F3
Boardman, OH 44512
Phone: (800) 207-4047
Fax: (800) 219-0213
e-mail: melody@dmci.net
essential oils and soap supplies

Soap Crafters Co.
363 East 3300 South, Ste. #5
Salt Lake City, UT 84115
Phone: (801) 484-5121
Fax: (801) 487-1958
fragrance oils and soap supplies

Sweet Cakes Fine Fragrance Oils
39 Brookdale Rd.
Bloomfield, NJ 07003
Phone: (201) 338-9830
Suprphat@aol.com

Oils, Molds, and Misc. Supplies

Appalachian Valley Natural Products
various regional distributors
www.AV-AT.com
essential oils, soap, and misc. supplies

Bear American Marketing
PO Box 829
Bear, DE 19701-0829
Phone: (302) 836-4187
e-mail: tlshay@magpage.com
wholesale: many soapmaking-related items

Boston Jojoba
PO Box 771
Middleton, MA 01949
Phone: (800) 256-5622
bob@bostonjojoba.com
jojoba oil, golden or deodorized

Changes Within
PO Box 326
Freeburg, PA 17827
Phone: (717) 374-6735
changes@sunlink.net

Columbus Foods Co.
800 North Albany
Chicago, IL 60622
Phone: (800) 322-6457
        or (773) 265-6500
Fax: (773) 265-6985
most vegetable oils

Creative Wholesale Dist.
164 Andrews Dr. #-400
Stockbridge, GA 30281-6366
Phone: (770) 474-2110
individual soap molds

Fuji Vegetable Oil, Inc.
20 Brampton Rd.
Savannah, GA 31408
Phone: (912) 966-5900
Fax: (912) 966-6913
fvonyk@aol.com
palm and other vegetable oils

Gentle Ridge
3655 Beaver Creek Dr.
Hillsboro, WI 54634-3038
Phone: toll free (877) 436-8537
        or (608) 489-3862
Fax: (608) 489-2432
emu oil

Gold Medal Products
10700 Medallion Dr.
Cincinnati, OH 45241-4807
Phone: (800) 543-0862
        or (513) 769-7676
Fax: toll free (800) 542-1496
e-mail: goldme19@eos.net
"white" coconut oil; often available via local distributors

Good Food
Phone: (800) 327-4406
        or (610) 273-7652
palm oil, coconut oil, canola oil, olive and pomace oils

Hagenow Laboratories, Inc.
1302 Washington St.
Manitowoc, WI 54220
lye, waxes, clays, essential oils, thermometers and pH kits

Lori, aka PigmntLady
PO Box 194
Old Saybrook, CT 06475
Phone: (860) 395-0085
cosmetic grade pigments, cutters

Majestic Mountain Sage
www.the-sage.com
online lye calculator and supplies

Milky Way Molds
4326 SE Woodstock, Ste. 473
Portland, OR 97206
Phone: (800) 588 7030
www.milkywaysoapmolds.com
individual soap molds and books

Nashville Wraps
Phone: (800) 547-9727
wrapping supplies of all types, catalog available

The Petal Pusher
PO Box 280
Silvana, WA 98287
Phone: (360) 652-4367
Petal@monroe.net
http://www.saponifier.com
The Saponifier, bimonthly trade magazine for soap and toiletry makers

Pourette Soapmaking Supplies
6910 Roosevelt Way NE
Seattle, WA 98115
Phone: (800) 888-WICK (9425)
www.pourette.com
molds, wax; request soapmaking price list

SKS Bottle & Packaging
3 Knabner Rd.
Mechanicsville, NY 12118
Phone: (518) 899-7488 Ext 308
Fax: (518) 899-7490
e-mail: ZEHNERE@AOL.COM
wide range of bottles, vials, and jars

Sunburst Bottle Co.
5710 Auburn Blvd., Ste. 7
Sacramento, CA 95841
Phone: (916) 348-5576
Fax: (916) 348-3803
sunburst@cwo.com
bottles and jars

TKB Trading
360 24th St.
Oakland, CA 94612
Phone: (510) 451-9011
www.tkbtrading.com
melt and pour soap base

Bibliography

The Encyclopedia of Herbs and Herbalism, Malcolm Stuart ed. Orbis Publishing, London 1979

The Aromatherapy Book: Applications & Inhalations, Jeanne Rose, Herbal Studies Course/Jeanne Rose and North Atlantic Books, Berkeley, CA 1992

The Essential Book of Herbal Medicine, Simon Y. Mills, Penguin Books, NY, NY, 1993.

Tea Tree Oil, a Medicine Kit in a Bottle, Susan Drury, C.W. Daniel Company, Ltd., Essex, England, 1992.

The Directory of Essential Oils, Wanda Sellar, C.W. Daniel Company, Ltd., Essex, England, 1992.

Taylor's Guide to Herbs, Rita Buchanan, ed., Houghton Mifflin Co., NY, NY, 1995.

The Natural Soap Book, Making Herbal and Vegetable-Based Soaps, Susan Miller Cavitch, Storey Publishing, Pownal, VT, 1995.

Aromatherapy, The Complete Guide to Plant and Flower Essences for Health and Beauty, Daniele Ryman, Bantam, NY, NY, 1993.

The Practice of Aromatherapy, Jean Valnet, M.D., Healing Arts Press, Rochester, VT, 1990.

The Soap Book, Simple Herbal Recipes, Sandy Maine, Interweave Press, Inc., Loveland, CO, 1995.

Scentsations, A Handbook for Fragrance Crafting, Nancy M. Booth, 1995.

Soap - Making It, Enjoying It, Ann Bramsom, 2nd ed., Workman Publishing Co., NY, NY, 1975.

Bath Scents, Alan Hayes, Angus & Robertson, NY, NY, 1994.

Soap Recipes, Seventy Tried-and-True Ways to Make Modern Soap with Herbs, Beeswax, and Vegetable Oils, Elaine C. White, Valley Hills Press, Starkville, MS, 1995.

Making Potpourri Colognes and Soaps, David A. Webb, Tab Books, Summit, PA, 1988.

The Complete Book of Herbs and Herb Growing, Roy Genders, Sterling Publishing Co., NY, NY, 1982.

The Illustrated Encyclopedia of Essential Oils, The Complete Guide to the Use of Oils in Aromatherapy and Herbalism, Julia Lawless, Element Books, Rockport, MA, 1995.

The Merck Index, 9th ed., M. Windholz, editor, Merck & Co., Inc., Rahway, NJ, 1976

Kirk-Othmer Concise Encyclopedia of Chemical Technology, D. Eckroth Ed., Wiley-Interscience, John Wiley & Sons, Inc., NY, 1985.

Bailey's Industrial Oil & Fat Products, Y. H. Hui editor, fifth edition, Wiley-Interscience, John Wiley & Sons, Inc., NY, 1996

Index

BE INSPIRED BY CREATIVE IDEAS

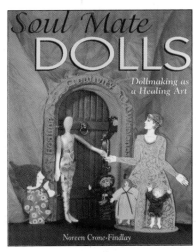

Treasures From The Earth
Creating With Flowers and Nature
by Kathy Lamancusa
Create something special from flowers and nature. Television personality Kathy Lamancusa explains how sources of inspiration can easily be found on a walk through the woods, a stroll by the ocean or a visit to the garden. She glorifies products found in nature with 75 projects.
Softcover • 8-1/4 x 10-7/8 • 160 pages
175 color photos • color illustrations
TREA • $22.95

Naturally Creative Candles
by Letty Oates
This unique art form is brought to vivid life as author Letty Oates demonstrates the immense potential of numerous natural materials in making and decorating different candles. More than 250 sharp photos reveal the results of creative candlemaking.
Softcover • 8-1/2 x 11 • 128 pages
250 color photos
NACC • $19.95

Modeling in Wax for Jewelry and Sculpture
2nd Edition
by Lawrence Kallenberg
You will be delighted when you finish your first piece of jewelry with the help of this definitive text on the ancient art of wax casting and mold-making. New breakthroughs in the casting process and new waxes and equipment are included as well as detailed instructions and illustrations of works in progress. Start to finish, the details are all here.
Softcover • 8-1/2 x 11 • 256 pages
16-page color section
MWJS2 • $34.95

Warman's Depression Glass
A Value & Identification Guide
by Ellen Schroy, Editor
Explore the timeless and very popular Depression Glass collectibles with this up-to-date guide containing descriptions and 9,600 values for nearly 140 patterns. Photos and drawings detail and identify the invaluable patterns such as Adam, Colonial, Jubilee, Old English, Patrick and Windsor.
Softcover • 8-1/2 x 10-7/8 • 224 pages
200 illustrations • 200 color photos
WDG01 • $24.95

Satisfaction Guarantee
If for any reason you are not completely satisfied with your purchase, simply return it within 14 days and receive a full refund, less shipping.

krause publications
700 E State St, Iola, WI 54990

Visit and order from our secure web site: www.krausebooks.com